T0230057

Lecture Notes in Artificial Intelligence (LNAI)

Other volumes of the Lecture Notes in Computer Science relevant to Artificial Intelligence:

Lecture Notes in Artificial Intelligence

Subseries of Lecture Notes in Computer Science
Edited by J. Siekmann

Lecture Notes in Computer Science

Edited by G. Goos and J. Hartmanis

Editorial

Artificial Intelligence has become a major discipline under the roof of Computer Science. This is also reflected by a growing number of titles devoted to this fast developing field to be published in our Lecture Notes in Computer Science. To make these volumes immediately visible we have decided to distinguish them by a special cover as Lecture Notes in Artificial Intelligence, constituting a subseries of the Lecture Notes in Computer Science. This subseries is edited by an Editorial Board of experts from all areas of AI, chaired by Jörg Siekmann, who are looking forward to consider further AI monographs and proceedings of high scientific quality for publication.

We hope that the constitution of this subseries will be well accepted by the audience of the Lecture Notes in Computer Science, and we feel confident that the subseries will be recognized as an outstanding opportunity for publication by authors and editors of the AI community.

Editors and publisher

Lecture Notes in Artificial Intelligence

Edited by J. Siekmann

Subseries of Lecture Notes in Computer Science

437

D. Kumar (Ed.)

Current Trends in SNePS – Semantic Network Processing System

First Annual SNePS Workshop
Buffalo, NY, November 13, 1989
Proceedings

Springer-Verlag

Berlin Heidelberg New York London Paris Tokyo Hong Kong

Editor

Deepak Kumar
Department of Computer Science, 226 Bell Hall
State University of New York at Buffalo
Buffalo, NY 14260, USA

CR Subject Classification (1987): I.2

ISBN 3-540-52626-9 Springer-Verlag Berlin Heidelberg New York
ISBN 0-387-52626-9 Springer-Verlag New York Berlin Heidelberg

Printing and binding: Druckhaus Beltz, Hemsbach/Bergstr.

Preface

The First Annual SNePS Workshop was held on November 13, 1989, at the State University of New York at Buffalo. SNePS is a state-of-the-art knowledge representation and reasoning system used for Artificial Intelligence and Cognitive Science research. It is a semantic network based system designed by members of the SNePS Research Group in conjunction with and under the supervision of Dr. Stuart C. Shapiro and Dr. William J. Rapaport. SNePS 2.1, an implementation of SNePS in Common Lisp, runs on several computers and is distributed under license from the Research Foundation of the State University of New York. The aims of this workshop were to bring together Artificial Intelligence researchers working with (or interested in) SNePS. Twelve research papers were presented by people from seven different research sites in the United States and abroad. The papers were of top quality and covered several areas of ongoing AI research displaying the versatility of SNePS as an AI research tool. The presentations were interspersed with several discussion sessions concerning achievements of the participants as a collective SNePS community and were helpful in outlining future research directions. This volume contains all the papers presented at the workshop.

Attendance at the workshop was by invitation only. It was attended by 46 participants from 14 different organizations and three different countries. The group from Instituto Superior Téchnico, University of Lisbon, is actively developing SNePS and its environments, and they brought new implementations of several systems, including a SNePS based theorem prover and a knowledge debugger. These are currently being incorporated in SNePS 2.1 and will be included in future distributions.

This workshop was sponsored by the SNePS Research Group and the SUNY at Buffalo Center for Cognitive Science.

Many thanks to the authors and participants for making the workshop a great success. Thanks to Sy Ali and Hans Chalupsky for taking charge of the various organizational chores. Thanks also to Eloise Benzel, Sally Elder, Gloria Koontz, Leslie Russo, and Lynda Spahr for providing administrative support. And thanks to Dr. William Rapaport and the SUNY at Buffalo Center for Cognitive Science for providing funding for the printing of an early version of these proceedings as a Department of Computer Science, SUNY at Buffalo, technical report. This volume contains revised and updated versions of the papers in the technical report.

Deepak Kumar
Buffalo, March 1990

Contents

Recent Advances and Developments: The SNePS 2.1 Report

Stuart C. Shapiro
SUNY at Buffalo
226 Bell Hall
Buffalo, NY 14260
(shapiro@cs.buffalo.edu)

João P. Martins
Instituto Superior Técnico
Av. Rovisco Pais
1000 Lisboa, Portugal
(ist_1416@ptifm.bitnet)

Abstract

In this paper, we describe those features that distinguish SNePS 2.1 from earlier versions of SNePS. These include: contexts; belief spaces; the knowledge debugger; the graphics package; and the elimination of duplicated reports. We also describe the SNePS 2.1 versions of path-based inference and SNePSLOG, and, finally, we indicate areas of SNePS 2.1 that still need work.

1 Introduction

SNePS 2.1 relies on the notion of belief. By *belief* we mean a proposition which can satisfy an antecedent of a rule. We are usually interested in a set of believed propositions. When SNePS 2.1 considers another one of these sets we say that it *changes its beliefs*. One important aspect related with the concept of belief is the reason for holding the belief. (We are only interested in *justified belief*, where the justification is either that the proposition has been entered by an outside system, typically a SNePS user—these are called hypotheses—or that the proposition follows from other beliefs—including rules—by the rules of inference of SNIP, the SNePS Inference Package.) Reasons for holding beliefs, called *justifications for beliefs* or *supports for beliefs*, are generated by SNePS 2.1 itself. SNePS 2.1 is able to detect contradictions, identify possible culprits for the contradictions, and to revise its beliefs in order to remove contradictions.

2 SWM

Any logic underlying a belief revision system has to keep track of and propagate propositional dependencies. This is important, because, in the event of the detection of a contradiction, we should be able to identify *exactly which* assumptions were used in the derivation of the contradictory propositions.

SWM deals with objects called *supported wffs*. A supported wff consists of a wff and an associated triple, its *support*, containing an *origin tag*, an *origin set*, and a *restriction set*. We write $<A, \tau, \alpha, \rho>$ to denote that A is a wff with origin tag τ, origin set α, and restriction set ρ, and we define the functions $wff(<A, \tau, \alpha, \rho >)=A$, $ot(<A, \tau, \alpha, \rho >)=\tau$, $os(<A, \tau, \alpha, \rho >)=\alpha$ and $rs(<A, \tau, \alpha,$

$\rho >$)$=\rho$. Notice that the support is not part of the wff itself but rather associated with a *particular occurrence of the wff*. The set of all supported wffs is called the *knowledge base*.

The origin set is a set of hypotheses. The origin set of a supported wff contains those (and only those) hypotheses that were *actually used* in the derivation of that wff. The origin tags range over the set $\{hyp, der, ext\}$: *hyp* identifies hypotheses, *der* identifies normally derived wffs within SWM, and *ext* identifies special wffs whose origin set was extended.[1] A restriction set is a set of sets of hypotheses. A supported wff whose restriction set is $\{\Theta_1, \ldots, \Theta_n\}$ means that the hypotheses in its origin set added to any of the sets Θ_1, ..., Θ_n produce an *inconsistent set*. Restriction sets can be proved to be [Martins and Shapiro 88]:

- *Sound*, that is, $\forall r \in rs(< A, \tau, \alpha, \rho >), r \cup os(< A, \tau, \alpha, \rho >)$ is known to be inconsistent;

- *Minimal*, that is, $\forall\ r \in rs(< A, \tau, \alpha, \rho >)$, $(r \cap os(< A, \tau, \alpha, \rho >)) = \emptyset$ and $(\forall r,\ s \in rs(< A, \tau, \alpha, \rho >)) \wedge\ (r \neq s))\ r \not\subset s$;

- *Complete*, that is they contain information about every set *known to be inconsistent.*[2]

Furthermore, it can be shown that restriction sets are a function of origin sets alone and we sometimes write $< A, \tau, \alpha, RS(\alpha) >$ instead of $< A, \tau, \alpha, \rho >$.

The origin tag and origin set of a supported wff are related with a *particular derivation* of its wff whereas the restriction set reflects our current knowledge about how the hypotheses underlying this derivation relate to the other hypotheses in the knowledge base. Once a supported wff is generated, its origin tag and origin set remain constant; however, its restriction set changes as the knowledge about all the propositions in the knowledge base does.

3   Contexts and Belief Spaces

We now discuss how SWM's features can be used in applications of belief revision. We define the behavior of an abstract belief revision system. This system works with a knowledge base containing supported wffs (in SWM's sense). Supported wffs are added to the knowledge base according to the rules of inference of SWM.

We define a *context* to be a set of hypotheses (supported wffs whose origin tags are "*hyp*"). A context determines a *belief space* (BS), which is the set of all the hypotheses defining the context and all the supported wffs that were derived exclusively from them. Within the SWM formalism, the supported wffs in a given BS are characterized by having an origin set that is contained in the context.

---

[1] A supported wff with "*ext*" origin tag has to be treated specially in order to avoid the introduction of irrelevancies [Martins and Shapiro 88].

[2] It is important to distinguish between a set *being* inconsistent and a set *being known to be* inconsistent. An inconsistent set is one from which a contradiction *can be* derived; a set known to be inconsistent is an inconsistent set from which a contradiction *has been* derived. The goal of adding restriction sets is to avoid re-considering *known* inconsistent sets of hypotheses.

Any operation performed within this system (query, addition, etc.) is associated with a context. We refer to the context under consideration, i.e., the context associated with the operation currently being performed, as the *current context*. While the operation is being carried out, the only propositions that will be considered are the propositions in the BS defined by the current context. This BS will be called the *current belief space*. A proposition is said to be *believed* if it belongs to the current BS.

4   SNePS 2.1

SNePS 2.1 [Shapiro, *et al.* 89] is a particular implementation of the abstract system of Section 3 within SNePS [Shapiro 79, Shapiro and Rapaport 87]. This section discusses some of the specifics of this implementation.

4.1   Contexts in SNEPS 2.1

A SNePS 2.1 *context* is a structure with three components: 1) a set of hypotheses; 2) a restriction set; 3) a set of names. The set of hypotheses is a set of nodes which are the assumptions of the context. The set of hypotheses is the determining component of the context in the sense that no two contexts will have the same set of hypotheses. The restriction set is a set of sets of nodes, such that the union of any of these sets with the set of hypotheses in the context forms a set of hypotheses from which a contradiction has been derived (*i.e.* a set of hypotheses known to be inconsistent). The set of names is a set of symbols each of which functions as a name of this context.

A context name intensionally defines a context, which is extensionally defined by its set of hypotheses. The SNePSUL user always refers to contexts by name, and may add assertions to, or remove assertions from a context. Actually, such changes do not change contexts (extensionally defined), but change context that the name refers to. The system takes care of such details, and the SNePSUL user may normally think of context name as always referring to the same context.

The user is always working in a particular context, called the *current context*. The current context for a particular SNePSUL command may be specified by an optional argument to the command. Otherwise, all commands are carried out with the *default context* as current context. By default, this context is named **default-defaultct**.

In SNePS 2.1, a proposition node is not simply asserted or unasserted—it is either asserted or unasserted in each context. A node name will be suffixed with ! when that node is asserted in the current context. An *hypothesis* is a node that was asserted by the user using **assert** or !, rather than being asserted only because it was derived during inference. An hypothesis is always an hypothesis of one or more context; it may also be asserted in other contexts, and might be unasserted in still other contexts.

Every node is said to be *in* zero or more contexts. A node n is in a context c in any of the following cases:

- n is one of the hypotheses that define c.

- n has been derived from a set of assumptions that is a subset of the set of hypotheses of c.

• *n* is dominated by a node in *c*.

4.2   Context Specifiers

The following SNePSUL commands allow an optional *context-specifier* argument in SNePS 2.1: assert; add; !; dump; describe; full-describe; find (and all its variations); and deduce. full-describe is a new command in SNePS 2.1. It is like describe, but also prints all the support information of the argument node(s). The syntax of *context-specifier*, and what context is specified by each possibility is:

omit
> If the *context-specifier* is omitted, the specified context is the default context (the value of *defaultct).

:context
> The context specified is the default context (the value of *defaultct).

:context *context-name*
> The context specified is that named *context-name*, which must be a symbol.

:context *nodeset context-name*
> The context specified is that named *context-name* which is initialized to be the context whose set of hypotheses is the value of *nodeset*, which must be a SNePSUL expression that evaluates to a set of proposition nodes.

:context all-hyps
> The context specified is the one whose set of hypotheses is the set of all hypotheses—all assertions entered by the user.

4.3   Operating on Contexts

The commands added to SNePS 2.1 for operating on contexts are:

(set-context *nodeset [symbol]*)
> Creates a context whose hypothesis set is *nodeset* (which cannot contain pattern nodes). If symbol is given, that is made the name of the context; otherwise *defaultct becomes the name of the context.

(set-default-context *context-name*)
> Changes the default context (the value of *defaultct) to be *context-name*.

(add-to-context *nodeset [context-name]*)
> Adds the nodes of *nodeset* into the hypothesis set of the context, *context-name*. If *context-name* is omitted, adds the hypotheses to *defaultct.

(remove-from-context *nodeset [context-name]*)
> Removes the nodes of *nodeset* from the hypothesis set of the context, *context-name*. If *context-name* is omitted, removes the hypotheses from *defaultct.

(list-context-names)
> Prints a list of all valid context names.

(describe-context *[context-name]*)
> Prints the hypothesis set, restriction set, and all names of the context named *context-name*. If *context-name* is omitted, prints the information on *defaultct.

(list-hypotheses *[context-name]*)
> Returns the hypothesis set of the context named *context-name*. If *context-name* is omitted, returns the hypothesis set of *defaultct.

5 Path-Based Inference

Path-based inference allows the inference of the existence of an arc between two nodes based on the existence of a path of arcs between those nodes. Path-based inference has been used in SNePS for years. When SNePS 2.1 was introduced, path-based inference remained implemented, but nodes inferred by path-based inference did not have reliable supports, because no study had been done to decide how to compute them. Path-based inference did, however, take belief spaces into account in that the ! operator checked for assertion in the current belief space.

An approach to defining the support of nodes inferred by path-based inference in SNePS 2.1 was taken by [Cravo and Martins 89a] and fully implemented. A path-based inference rule is of the form $<r> \leftarrow <P>$. Where $< r >$ is an arc and $< P >$ is a $< path >$. This approach allows the user to do the same inferences as before, except for those involving paths that rely on the non-existence of a path between two nodes.[3] It is now the user's responsibility to specify which nodes should be taken into account for the computation of the support of the inferred node.

In [Cravo and Martins 89a] we specify how the support of the inferred node should be computed. The support will depend on (1) The support of the node from which the path was found; (2) The specification of the followed path; and, (3) The supports of some of the nodes the path went through.

6 SNePSLOG

SNePSLOG is a logic-based interface to SNePS and was first proposed by [McKay and Martins 81]. During the last year a new version was SNePSLOG was developed [Matos and Martins 89]. This new version contemplates contexts and belief spaces and and example of its usage follows (this is a slightly edited version of the interaction—some of the inferences are not presented and the description of contexts is edited, it will be done in this way in the near future):

---

[3]There are some paths that were allowed in SNePS 2.0 and are not allowed in SNePS 2.1, those that rely on the lack of existence of some paths; they were not considered because SWM is a monotonic logic.

```
: White(Pegasus)
  WFF1: WHITE(PEGASUS) {<HYP, {WFF1}, {}>}

: Horse(Tornado)
  WFF2: HORSE(TORNADO) {<HYP, {WFF2}, {}>}

: all(x) (Horse(x) => ~Flies(x))
  WFF3: ALL(X)(HORSE(X) => (~FLIES(X))) {<HYP, {WFF3}, {}>}

: all(x) (Winged-Horse(x) => Flies(x))
  WFF4: ALL(X)(WINGED-HORSE(X) => FLIES(X)) {<HYP, {WFF4}, {}>}

: all(x) (Winged-Horse(x) => Horse(x))
  WFF5: ALL(X)(WINGED-HORSE(X) => HORSE(X)) {<HYP, {WFF5}, {}>}

: all(x) (Winged-Horse(x) => Has-Wings(x))
  WFF6: ALL(X)(WINGED-HORSE(X) => HAS-WINGS(X)) {<HYP, {WFF6}, {}>}

: Winged-Horse(Pegasus)
  WFF7: WINGED-HORSE(PEGASUS) {<HYP, {WFF7}, {}>}
```

The interaction above created supported wffs corresponding to propositions WFF1 through WFF7. Now we initiate backward inference, trying to determine "who flies".

```
: Flies(?Who) ?

I wonder if FLIES(?WHO)
holds within the BS defined by context
{WFF1 WFF2 WFF3 WFF4 WFF5 WFF6 WFF7}

I wonder if WINGED-HORSE(X)
holds within the BS defined by context
{WFF1 WFF2 WFF3 WFF4 WFF5 WFF6 WFF7}

I Know WINGED-HORSE(PEGASUS) {<HYP, {WFF7}, {}>}

Since ALL(X)(WINGED-HORSE(X) => FLIES(X)) {<HYP, {WFF4}, {}>}
and WINGED-HORSE(PEGASUS) {<HYP, {WFF7}, {}>}
I infer FLIES(PEGASUS)

Since ALL(X)(WINGED-HORSE(X) => HORSE(X)) {<HYP, {WFF5}, {}>}
and WINGED-HORSE(PEGASUS) {<HYP, {WFF7}, {}>}
I infer HORSE(PEGASUS)
```

```
Since ALL(X)(HORSE(X) => (~FLIES(X))) {<HYP, {WFF3}, {}>}
and HORSE(PEGASUS) {<DER. {WFF7, WFF5}, {} >}
I infer ~FLIES(PEGASUS)
```

```
A contradiction has been found. The propositions involved are
WFF12: ~FLIES(PEGASUS) and WFF8: FLIES(PEGASUS).
```

At this point the user will get into an interactive package that enables the inspection of the hypotheses underlying the contradictory wffs, the inspection of the other hypotheses in the current belief space, and the removal of any of them. This package is described in the next section. In our example we decided to remove hypothesis WFF4, and the inference proceeds. Note that ~FLIES(TORNADO) and ~FLIES(PEGASUS) were derived in the previous BS and still hold in the new one, and thus are not re-derived.

```
The contradiction has been solved by removing the hypothesis WFF4
```

```
I wonder if FLIES(?WHO)
holds within the BS defined by context
{WFF1 WFF2 WFF3 WFF5 WFF6 WFF7}
```

```
I Know ~FLIES(TORNADO) {<DER, {WFF3, WFF2}, {{WFF7, WFF5, WFF4}}>}
```

```
I Know ~FLIES(PEGASUS) {<DER. {WFF7, WFF5, WFF3}, {{WFF4}}>}
```

```
WFF10: ~FLIES(TORNADO) {<DER. {WFF3, WFF2}, {{WFF7, WFF5, WFF4}}>}
WFF12: ~FLIES(PEGASUS) {<DER. {WFF7, WFF5, WFF3}, {{WFF4}} >}
```

7   The Knowledge Debugger

The knowledge debugger is an interactive package used to remove hypotheses from a context when a contradiction is detected. The knowledge debugger offers an environment which is similar to the debugger existing in LISP Machines. The user can inspect extended wffs, find out the extended wffs that depend on a given hypothesis, remove hypotheses, or add new hypotheses to a context (see Figure 1).

8   Graphics Package

The graphics package is still under construction. Its goal is to enable a user to follow the process of inference in a graphical form rather than in a textual form that is traditionally done in SNePS. In Figure 2 we show part of the inference trace generated during the execution of the example in Section 6.

There are still outstanding problems to be solved in this area concerning and-entailments, and-ors, and threshes, changes in belief spaces, etc.

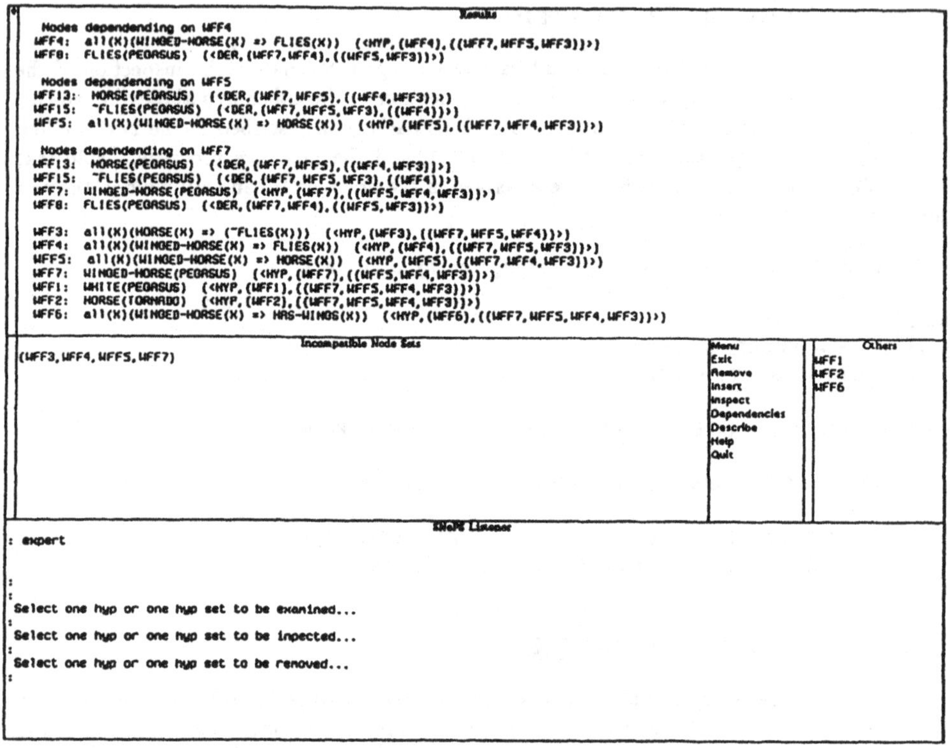

Figure 1: Interface to the knowledge debugger

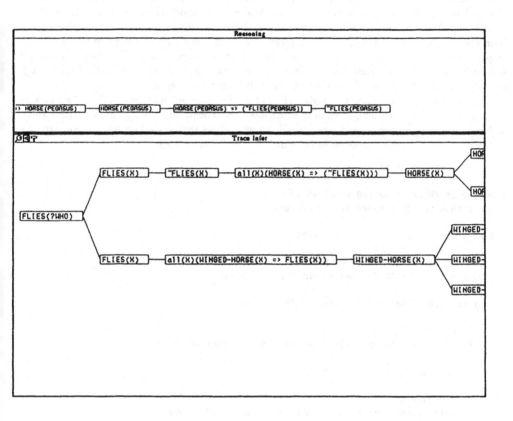

Figure 2: A sample trace of the reasoning

9   Theorem Proving

Unlike earlier versions of SNePS, SNePS 2.1 is capable of using the rules of Universal Generalization and of Entailment Introduction. Both of these use the hypothetical reasoning capability of SNePS 2.1 ([Martins 83] and [Martins and Shapiro 86]). Taking advantage of this, SNePS 2.1 has been used to prove several theorems from [Whitehead and Russell 10]. Each proof starts with an empty network. The interesting aspect about this is that theorems correspond to derived extended wffs with empty origin set, meaning that they are *universal truths*: once derived, a theorem belongs to every context, there is no way we can remove it from our belief spaces.

The proof of one of the laws of syllogism (PC21 from [Whitehead and Russell 10]) is the following (again, there was some minor editing in this example—the indentation when we expand the context, and some extra inference reports were added, namely those that state Let me try to use the rule.... This will be incorporated in SNePSLOG in the near future):

```
: (p => q) => ((q => r) => (p => r)) ?

I wonder if (P => Q) => ((Q => R) => (P => R))
holds within the BS defined by the context ()

Let me assume that P => Q {<HYP, {WFF1}, {}>}

  I wonder if (Q => R) =>(P => R)
  holds within the BS defined by the context (WFF1)

  Let me assume that Q => R {<HYP, {WFF2}, {}>}

    I wonder if P => R
    holds within the BS defined by the context (WFF1 WFF2)

    Let me assume that P  {<HYP, {P}, {}>}

      I wonder if R
      holds within the BS defined by the context (WFF1 WFF2 P)

      Let me try to use the rule Q => R

      I wonder if Q
      holds within the BS defined by the context (WFF1 WFF2 P)

      Let me try to use the rule P => Q

      I know P  {<HYP, {P}, {}>}

      Since P => Q  {<HYP, {WFF1}, {}>}
      and P         {<HYP, {P}, {}>}
```

```
      I infer Q      {<DER, {WFF1, P}, {}>}

      Since Q => R  {<HYP, {WFF2}, {}>}
      and Q         {<DER, {WFF1, P}, {}>}
      I infer R     {<DER, {WFF1, WFF2, P}, {}>}

    Since R        {<DER, {WFF1, WFF2, P}, {}>}
    were derived under the assumption: P {<HYP, {P}, {}>}
    I infer P => R {<DER, {WFF1, WFF2}, {}>}

  Since P => R    {<DER, {WFF1, WFF2}, {}>}
  were derived under the assumption: Q => R {<HYP, {WFF2}, {}>}
  I infer (Q => R) => (P => R) {<DER, {WFF1}, {}>}

Since (Q => R) => (P => R) {<DER, {WFF1}, {}>}
were derived under the assumption: P => Q {<HYP, {WFF1}, {}>}
I infer P => Q => ((Q => R) => (P => R))  {<DER, {}, {}>}

(P => Q) => ((Q => R) => (P => R))  {<DER, {}, {}>}
```

Notice, again, that the proposition (P => Q) => ((Q => R) => (P => R)) has the following support (DER, {}, {}), meaning that it depends on *no* hypotheses.

10 Cutting Duplicated Reports

One problem that most SNePS users face, is the duplication of reports received during a deduction. Most of these duplications correspond to multiple derivations of the same proposition (which are important from the belief revision point of view). We modified SNIP so that only one report for each deduction is provided, although multiple derivations are carried out and recorded [Filipe 89].

11 Deficiencies of SNePS 2.1

The major current deficiencies of SNePS 2.1 are the lack of some of the features of earlier versions of SNIP. Specifically, default consequences, the non-derivable operator, numerical entailment, the existential quantifier, and the numerical quantifier have not yet been implemented. The problem with the existential quantifier is merely the lack of programming time, and we intend to add it as soon as time permits. The study of default consequences and the non-derivable operator is under way [Cravo and Martins 89b]. The implementation of numerical entailment awaits the solution of the semantic problem of how to count intentional entities that are coreferential.

Although the code for forward path-based inference has been written, it has not been included in the operations triggered by **add**. This, also, is merely a problem of programming time, although forward path-based inference was never included in earlier versions of SNePS.

12   Availability

SNePS 2.1, as discussed in this paper, is available for distribution under license from the Research Foundation of The State University of New York. Inquiries should be sent to the first author of this paper at the address given at the beginning of the paper.

13   Acknowledgements

Nuno Mamede and Hans Chalupsky were primarily responsible for incorporating SNeBR into the "official" copy of SNEPS 2.0 at SUNY at Buffalo, thereby creating SNePS 2.1. Maria R. Cravo studied and implemented path-based inference, and created the Flying Horses example described in Sections 6, 7, and 8. Carlos Pinto Ferreira initiated the study of SNePS as a theorem prover. Joaquim L. Filipe modified SNePS 2.1 to avoid duplicated reports. António Leitão participated in the development of the knowledge debugger and the graphics package. Pedro Amaro de Matos implemented SNePSLOG and participated in the development of the knowledge debugger and the graphics package. Sofia Pinto participated in the development of the knowledge debugger and the graphics package.

SNePS-2.1, as described in this paper, was supported in part by the following: the National Science Foundation under Grant IRI-8610517; the Defense Advanced Research Projects Agency under Contract F30602-87-C-0136 (monitored by the Rome Air Development Center) to the Calspan-UB Research Center; the Air Force Systems Command, Rome Air Development Center, Griffiss Air Force Base, New York 13441-5700, and the Air Force Office of Scientific Research, Bolling AFB DC 20332 under Contract No. F30602-85-C-0008, which supports the Northeast Artificial Intelligence Consortium (NAIC); Junta Nacional de Investigação Científica e Tecnológica (JNICT), under Grant 87-107; Instituto Nacional de Investigação Científica (INIC).

14   References

Cravo M.R. and Martins J.P., "Path-Based Inference Revisited", *Proc. First SNePS Workshop*, Heidelberg, W. Germany: Springer-Verlag, 1989a.

Cravo M.R. and Martins J.P., "Belief Revision with Defaults", submitted for publication, 1989b.

Filipe J.L., "A Solution for the Message Repetition Problem in SNePS", Technical Report 89/02, Lisbon, Portugal: Instituto Superior Técnico, Technical University of Lisbon, 1989.

Martins J.P., "Reasoning in Multiple Belief Spaces", Ph.D. Dissertation, Technical Report 203, Buffalo, N.Y.: Department of Computer Science, State University of New York at Buffalo, 1983.

Martins J.P. and Shapiro S.C., "Hypothetical Reasoning", *Proc. Applications of Artificial Intelligence to Engineering Problems*, Berlin, W. Germany: Springer-Verlag, pp.1029–1042, 1986.

Martins J.P. and Shapiro S.C., "A Model for Belief Revision", *Artificial Intelligence 35*, pp.25-79, 1988.

Matos P.A. and Martins J.P., "SNePSLOG - A logic Interface to SNePS", Technical Report 89/03, Lisbon, Portugal: Instituto Superior Técnico, Technical University of Lisbon, 1989.

McKay D.P. and Martins J.P., "SNePSLOG Users' Manual", SNeRG Technical Note 4, Buffalo, N.Y.: Department of Computer Science, State University of New York at Buffalo, 1981.

Shapiro S.C., "The SNePS Semantic Network Processing System", in *Associative Networks: Representation and Use of Knowledge by Computers*, Findler (ed.), New York, N.Y.: Academic Press, pp.179−203, 1979.

Shapiro S.C. et. al., SNePS-2 User's Manual, Buffalo, N.Y.: Department of Computer Science, State University of New York at Buffalo, 1989.

Shapiro S.C. and Rapaport W., "SNePS Considered as a Fully Intensional Propositional Semantic Network", in *The Knowledge Frontier: Essays in the Representation of Knowledge*, McCalla and Cercone (eds.), New York, N.Y.: Springer-Verlag, pp.262−315, 1987.

Whitehead A.N. and Russell B., *Principia Mathematica*, Cambridge, UK: Cambridge University Press, 1910 (2nd Edition, reprinted 1987).

PATH-BASED INFERENCE REVISITED

Maria R. Cravo and **João P. Martins**
Instituto Superior Técnico
Technical University of Lisbon
Av. Rovisco Pais
1000 Lisboa, Portugal

Abstract

Path-based inference allows the inference of the existence of an arc between two nodes based on the existence of a path of arcs between those nodes. Path-based inference has been used in the SNePS Semantic Network Processing System for several years. When SNePS was extended to include belief revision (giving rise to SNePS 2.1) the path-based inference capability was lost, because no study had been done to decide how to compute the dependency (on other nodes) of the node generated by path-based inference. In this paper we discuss how path-based inference was incorporated in SNePS 2.1 and show how to compute the dependency of the nodes generated by path-based inference.

1 Introduction

SNePS 2.1 is the latest version of SNePS [Shapiro and Rapaport 87] and includes a belief revision package, based on the logic SWM [Martins and Shapiro 88]. In SNePS 2.1 we can introduce hypotheses, reason from them, and, whenever a contradiction is derived SNePS 2.1 identifies those (and only those) hypotheses that underly the contradiction. Up to now the only inference allowed in SNePS 2.1 was node-based, i.e., the inference proceeds according to patterns of nodes.

In this paper we discuss path-based inference in SNePS 2.1 (inference that relies on the existence of a path between nodes) and compare it with a previous study [Cravo and Martins 89]. Path-based inference, although less general than node-based inference, is much more efficient. The main issue in the integration of path-based inference in SNePS 2.1 concerns the computation of the hypotheses that underly a newly generated node.

The structure of the paper is as follows: First we present some fundamental concepts of SWM; we discuss SNePS 2.1 and discuss node-based inference; we discuss path-based inference; we present a first attempt to introduce path-based inference in SNePS 2.1 and point out some of the problems associated with this approach; we discuss the process of computation of the hypotheses associated with a newly derived node using path-based inference; and, finally, we present an example of path-based inference.

2   SWM

SWM is a logic developed to support belief revision systems [Martins and Shapiro 88]. One of the main issues in these systems is the identification of dependencies among propositions; this is important because once a contradiction is detected we want to find out *exactly* which hypotheses underly the contradictory propositions.

SWM associates each derivation of a proposition with three items: an origin tag, an origin set, and a restriction set. The *origin tag* tells how the proposition was derived. An origin tag can either be "hyp" if the proposition was introduced as a hypothesis; "der" if it was normally derived; or "ext" if it was derived in a special way; The *origin set* contains exactly those hypotheses that underly the derivation of the proposition. The origin set is computed whenever a proposition is derived; The *restriction set* contains those sets of hypotheses that are known to be incompatible with the proposition's origin set. These sets are propagated through the application of rules of inference and are updated whenever contradictions are detected.

SWM deals with supported wffs which are of the form $< A, \tau, \alpha, \rho >$, where A is a wff, τ its origin tag, α its origin set, and ρ its restriction set. The triple (τ, α, ρ) is called the support of the wff A. If the same wff is derived in several different ways there will be several supported wffs with the same wff and we say that the wff has different supports.

It can be shown that the restriction set of a supported wff is a function of its origin set alone and therefore two supported wffs with the same origin set have the same restriction set [Martins and Shapiro 88]. For this reason, in this paper we will not be concerned with the computation of the restriction sets and we will write supported wffs as $< A, \tau, \alpha, RS(\alpha) >$, where $RS(\alpha)$ stands for the restriction set associated with the origin set α.

The rules of inference of SWM make use of functions that compute the origin tag, origin set, and restriction set of the derived supported wffs. For the purpose of this paper we mention just one of them, Λ, that takes as arguments the origin tags of two or more supported wffs to be combined by a rule of inference and produces the origin tag of the resulting supported wff. Its description can be found in [Martins and Shapiro 88].

3   SNePS 2.1 – SNePS with Belief Revision

In SNePS 2.1 there are nodes, arcs, and supports. *Nodes* represent concepts; *Arcs* represent non-conceptual relations between concepts; *Supports*, are associated with every node that represents a proposition, and correspond to the proposition's support(s) in SWM's sense.[1]

In Figure 1 we show some objects in SNePS 2.1. In this figure, M1 represents the proposition that "Rover is a dog". This proposition is associated with the support (hyp, {M1}, $RS(\{M1\})$) which is shown close to node M1. The arcs member and class are forward arcs (relations). Besides these arcs, there exist reverse arcs labeled member- from Rover to M1 and class- from dogs to M1. Something similar holds for node M2 that represents the proposition that "dogs are mammals".

---

[1]Since propositions are represented by nodes, a given node may have more than one support, if the corresponding proposition was derived in more than one way.

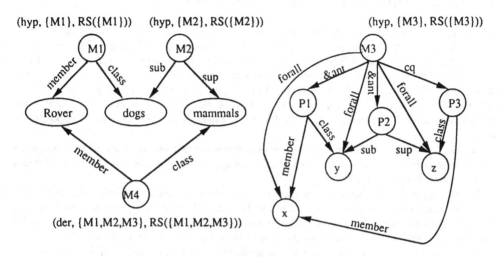

Figure 1: Example of nodes in SNePS 2.1

Node M3 represents the proposition "if someone is a member of a class and that class is contained in a superclass then that someone is also a member of the superclass". ¿From nodes M1, M2, and M3, SNePS 2.1 is able to deduce (using node-based inference) that "Rover is a mammal" (node M4) and associates it with the support (der, {M1, M2, M3}, $RS(\{M1,M2,M3\})$) (see Figure 1). The inference is node-based because it proceeds according to the existence of instances of patterns of nodes: P1 which is in antecedent position of a rule matches M1 with the substitution {x/Rover, y/dogs}, P2 which is also in antecedent position of the rule, matches M2 with the substitution {y/dogs, z/mammals} and thus we may infer an instance of the pattern P3 with the substitution {x/Rover, y/dogs, z/mammals} (node M4).

4 Path-Based Inference

The result obtained at the end of the previous section could have been obtained in a rather different way: Suppose that we have nodes M1 and M2 of Figure 1 and that we tell SNePS 2.1 that whenever the sequence of arcs member-/class/sub-/super is found from a node x to a node y then it can infer the existence of the sequence of arcs member-/class from node x to node y; under these circumstances SNePS 2.1 could infer node M4 of Figure 1.

However, the way M4 is derived is very different from the previous derivation: rather than relying on the existence of instances of patterns of nodes we rely on the existence of a sequence of arcs (which we call a *path*) from a node to another, this is *path-based inference* [Shapiro 78], [Srihari 81].

5 First Approach to Path-Based Inference

A first approach to defining path-based inference in SNePS 2.1 was taken by [Cravo and Martins 89]. In this approach, the standard SNePS2.0 syntax for defining paths ([Shapiro 78], [Srihari 81]) was dropped in favour of the following: a path-based inference rule was of the form $(<R_1 >, <R_2 >)$ $\leftarrow$ <path> where $<R_1 >$ and $<R_2 >$ are forward arcs and <path> is a path. ¿From this rule, and the existence of the path <path> from node x to node y we could infer a new node with arc $<R_1 >$ to x and arc $<R_2 >$ to y. In an informal way, the path described in Section 4 could be specified as (member, class) $\leftarrow$ member- / class / sub- / super, where "/" represents composition of arcs.

Formally, a <path> was either the sequence of a reverse arc followed by a forward arc (elementary path) or was formed in some of the ways defined in [Shapiro et. al. 89] (some of the ways of forming paths are also described in Section 6).

In this approach two main modifications were made to the previous SNePS2.0 syntax of path-based inference rules. The first one concerns the definition of elementary path: it is no longer any arc, but the composition of a reverse with a forward arc. The second modification requires the left hand side of a path-based inference rule to be constituted by two relations, instead of just one.

The reasons for our proposal were: First, in predicate logic, propositions are inferred from other propositions not from parts of propositions. This was the reason behind the requirement that the elementary path must be the composition of a reverse arc with a forward arc, instead of a single arc (reverse or forward). In the last situation, as Shapiro says "Path-based inference involves the inferring of an arc between two nodes from the existence of a path of arcs between the same two nodes. Since this inference ignores the other arcs emanating from the starting node, it corresponds to an inference rule that ignores the arity of atomic propositions. This is not a situation that occurs in the standard syntax of predicate logic." [Shapiro 89a].

As to the result of an inference, again we can only, in predicate logic, infer propositions, the simplest ones being atomic propositions, and not parts of atomic propositions. This was the reason for requiring that the left hand side of a path-based inference rule be composed by two relations, connecting the two nodes at the ends of a path, and not just one relation.

The drawback of this approach is that it prevents path-based inference from being used in many situations where SNePS' users find it useful [Shapiro 89b]. The present approach allows the user to do the same inferences as before, except for those involving paths that rely on the non-existence of a path between two nodes. It is now the user's responsibility to specify which nodes should be taken into account for the computation of the support of the inferred node.

6 A Revised Approach

We now discuss the revised approach to path-based inference. A path-based inference rule is of the form <r> $\leftarrow$ <P>. Where $< r >$ is a relation (forward arc) and $< P >$ is a $<$ path $>$ as defined below. A path-based inference rule is defined by the SNePSUL command **define-path** whose syntax is (define-path <r> <P>).

In the present work we allow the definition of the following paths (their description was taken from [Shapiro et. al. 89]):[2]

1. <path> ::= < unitpath >
   Where < unitpath > is any single arc, either reverse or forward;

2. <path> ::= (converse <path>)
   If P is a <path> from node x to node y then (converse P) is a <path> from y to x;

3. <path> ::= (compose <path>*)
   If n_1, ... n_n are nodes and P_i is a <path> from node n_i to node n_{i+1} $(1 \leq i \leq n-1)$, then (compose P_1 ... P_{n-1}) is a path from n_1 to n_n. If the symbol "!" appears between P_{i-1} and P_i, then n_i must be asserted;

4. <path> ::= (kstar <path>)
   If path P composed with itself zero or more times is a path from node x to node y, then (kstar P) is a path from x to y;

5. <path> ::= (kplus <path>)
   If path P composed with itself one or more times is a path from node x to node y, then (kplus P) is a path from x to y;

6. <path> ::= (or {<path>}*)
   If P_1 is a path from node x to node y, or P_2 is a path from node x to node y, or ... or P_n is a path from node x to node y, then (or P_1 P_2 ... P_n) is a path from x to y;

7. <path> ::= (and {<path>}*)
   If P_1 is a path from node x to node y, and P_2 is a path from node x to node y, and ... and P_n is a path from node x to node y, then (and P_1 P_2 ... P_n) is a path from x to y;

8. <path> ::= (irreflexive-restrict {<path>}*)
   If P is a path from node x to node y, and x $\neq$ y, then (irreflexive-restrict P) is a path from x to y;

9. <path> ::= (domain-restrict (<path> <node>) <path>)
   If P is a path from node x to node y and Q is a path from node x to node z, then (domain-restrict (Q z) P) is a path from x to z;

10. <path> ::= (range-restrict <path> (<path> <node>))
    If P is a path from node x to node y and Q is a path from node y to node z, then (range-restrict P (Q z)) is a path from x to y.

---

[2]There are some paths that were allowed in SNePS2.0 and are not allowed in SNePS 2.1, those that rely on the lack of existence of some paths; they were not considered because SWM is a monotonic logic.

The definition (`define-path <r> <P>`) allows SNePS 2.1 to infer the existence of the relation r between a node x and a node y, from the existence of path P between those nodes.

We now specify how the support of the inferred node should be computed. The support will depend on (1) The support of the node from which the path was found; (2) The specification of the followed path; and, (3) The supports of some of the nodes the path went through.

Before proceeding, we define some functions used to compute the support of nodes generated by path-based inference.[3]

- *Support(node)*: Returns the support of *node*, a triple $(\tau, \alpha, RS(\alpha))$.

- *Contrib(path)*: Returns zero or more supports, which represent the contribution of *path* to the support of the inferred node. This may depend on the supports of some of the nodes *path* goes through.

- *AndSups($sup_1, sup_2, ...sup_n$)*: Receives as arguments an any number of supports and computes a support. If for $1 \leq i \leq n$ we have $sup_i = (\tau_i, \alpha_i, RS(\alpha_i))$, then the value of *AndSups($sup_1, sup_2, ...sup_n$)* will be $(\Lambda(\tau_1, \tau_2, ...\tau_n), \alpha_1 \cup \alpha_2 \cup ... \cup \alpha_n, RS(\alpha_1 \cup \alpha_2 \cup ... \cup \alpha_n))$. If $n = 1$, then $AndSups((\tau, \alpha, RS(\alpha))) = (\Lambda(\tau, \tau), \alpha, RS(\alpha))$.

Suppose that following the execution of (`define-path r P`) SNePS 2.1 could find in the network path P from a node, which we call the *StartNode* to another node, which we call the *EndNode*. In this case, SNePS 2.1 will be able to infer a new node, which we call the *InferredNode*; *InferredNode* will be the same as the *StartNode* except that path P from *StartNode* to *EndNode* will be substituted by relation r from *InferredNode* to *EndNode*. The support of *InferredNode* will be given by *AndSups(Support(StartNode), Contrib(P))*. The value of *Contrib(P)* depends on the way P is formed:

1. If P = s, where s is an arc, then *Contrib*(P) is *nil*.

2. If P is (`converse Q`) then *Contrib*(P) = *Contrib*(Q).

3. If P is (`compose P`$_1$ ... P$_n$) then *Contrib*(P) = *AndSups(Contrib(P$_1$), ..., Contrib(P$_n$), {Support(x) : x ∈ Ξ})*.[4] Where P_i is a path from node x_i to node x_{i+1} (for $1 \leq i \leq n$) and Ξ is the following set $\Xi = \{x_i$:the symbol "!" appears between P_{i-1} and $P_i\}$.

4. If P is (`kstar Q`) then *Contrib*(P) = *AndSups(C$_1$, ..., C$_n$)*, where n is the number of times that Q was composed with itself $(n \geq 0)$, and C_i = *Contrib*(Q) on the i-th time that Q was composed with itself.

5. If P is (`kplus Q`) then *Contrib*(P) = *AndSups(C$_1$, ..., C$_n$)*, where n is the number of times that Q was composed with itself $(n \geq 1)$, and C_i = *Contrib*(Q) on the i-th time that Q was composed with itself.

---

[3]Whenever a node has more than one support the procedures described below should be repeated for each support.

[4]Note that the arguments of this function are the *Contrib*(P$_i$) $(1 \leq i \leq n)$ and the elements of the set Ξ, not the set itself.

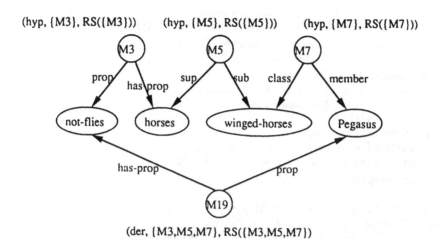

(der, {M3,M5,M7}, RS({M3,M5,M7})

Figure 2: Node M19 is generated by path-based inference

6. If P is (or P_1 ... P_n) then $Contrib(P) = Contrib(P_i)$, for each P_i that was found between *StartNode* and *EndNode*.

7. If P is (and P_1 ... P_n) then $Contrib(P) = AndSups(Contrib(P_1), ..., Contrib(P_n))$.

8. If P is (irreflexive-restrict Q) then $Contrib(P) = Contrib(Q)$.

9. If P is (domain-restrict (Q z) R) then
   $Contrib(P) = AndSups(Contrib(Q), Contrib(R))$.

10. If P is (range-restrict R (Q z)) then
    $Contrib(P) = AndSups(Contrib(Q), Contrib(R))$.

For example, suppose that the network contains the nodes M3, M5, and M7 shown in Figure 2 and that the command

```
(define-path has-prop (compose has-prop
                       (kstar (compose sup- ! sub))
                       (kstar (compose class- ! member))))
```

has been executed. In this situation, SNePS 2.1 would be able to infer, using path-based inference, node M19 (Figure 2). Let's see how the support of M19 was computed. This node was inferred because a path as specified in the command define-path was found between nodes M3 and Pegasus. In this case, we have

$Support(\text{M19}) = AndSups(Support(\text{M3}),$
$\qquad\qquad\qquad Contrib((\text{compose has-prop}$
$\qquad\qquad\qquad\qquad (\text{kstar (compose sup- ! sub)})$
$\qquad\qquad\qquad\qquad (\text{kstar (compose class- !}$
$\qquad\qquad\qquad\qquad \text{member}))))))$

$Contrib((\text{compose has-prop}$
$\qquad\qquad (\text{kstar (compose sup- ! sub)})$
$\qquad\qquad (\text{kstar (compose class- !}$
$\qquad\qquad \text{member})))) =$
$AndSups(Contrib(\text{has-prop}),$
$\qquad Contrib((\text{kstar(compose sup- ! sub)})),$
$\qquad Contrib((\text{kstar(compose class- ! member})))$

$Contrib(\text{has-prop})$ is *nil*

$Contrib((\text{kstar(compose sup- ! sub)})) =$
$AndSups(Contrib((\text{compose sup- ! sub})))^5 =$
$AndSups(AndSups(Contrib(\text{sup-}), Contrib(\text{sub}), Support(\text{M5}))) =$
$AndSups(AndSups(Support(\text{M5}))) = (\text{der, } \{\text{M5}\}, RS(\{\text{M5}\}))$

$Contrib((\text{kstar(compose class- ! member)})) =$
$AndSups(Contrib((\text{compose class- ! member})))^6 =$
$AndSups(AndSups(Contrib(\text{class-}), Contrib(\text{member}), Support(\text{M7}))) =$
$AndSups(AndSups(Support(\text{M7}))) = (\text{der, } \{\text{M7}\}, RS(\{\text{M7}\}))$

$Support(\text{M19}) =$
$AndSups(Support(\text{M3}),$
$\qquad AndSups((\text{der, } \{\text{M5}\}, RS(\{\text{M5}\})),$
$\qquad\qquad (\text{der, } \{\text{M7}\}, RS(\{\text{M7}\})))) =$
$AndSups((\text{der, } \{\text{M3}\}, RS(\{\text{M3}\})),$
$\qquad (\text{der, } \{\text{M5, M7}\}, RS(\{\text{M5,M7}\}))) =$
$(\text{der, } \{\text{M3, M5, M7}\}, RS(\{\text{M3,M5,M7}\})).$

7 Example

In this section we present an example. There are three aspects that we want to stress with this example: First the computation of the support of nodes generated by path-based inference; Second, the interaction between path-based and node-based inference; and Third, the interaction with the belief revision aspect of SNePS 2.1.

We assume that nodes M1, M2, M3, M4, M5, M6, and M7 shown in Figure 3 have been created as

---

[5]Path (compose sup- ! sub) was composed one time with itself.
[6]Path (compose class- ! member) was composed one time with itself.

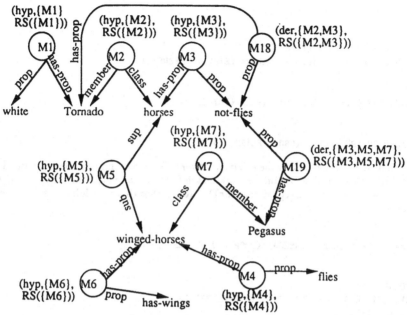

Figure 3: Nodes in SNePS 2.1

hypotheses. We also assume that there is one node (node M8) that corresponds to the node-based inference rule created by the command:[7]

```
(assert forall $x
        ant (build has-prop *x prop not-flies)
        cq  (build min 0 max 0 (build has-prop *x prop flies)))
```

This rule states that if something has the property not-flies then it does not have the property flies.

Furthermore, we assume that the following definition was given:

```
(define-path has-prop (compose has-prop
                               (kstar (compose sup- ! sub))
                               (kstar (compose class- ! member))))
```

The following is a slightly edited version of the trace produced during inference. Editing was done to remove extra inference reports that are not relevant for the presentation of this paper. Lowercase strings, following the * prompt, represent user input; uppercase strings represent SNePS 2.1 output.

```
* (full-describe (deduce has-prop $who prop flies))
```

---
[7]This node is not shown in Figure 3.

```
I wonder if
((P4 (HAS-PROP V2) (PROP (FLIES))))
holds within the BS defined by context DEFAULT-DEFAULTCT

I know
((M4! (HAS-PROP (WINGED-HORSES)) (PROP (FLIES))))

I know
((M9! (HAS-PROP (PEGASUS)) (PROP (FLIES))))
```

Notice that node M9 was not in the original network. This node has just been created by path-based inference. This was done by the network match function, when looking for nodes that match the pattern (P4 (has-prop V2)(prop (flies))). Remember that a path has been defined for the arc has-prop.

```
I know
((M10! (HAS-PROP (WINGED-HORSES)) (PROP (NOT-FLIES))))

Since
((M8! (FORALL V1)
      (ANT (P1 (HAS-PROP V1) (PROP (NOT-FLIES))))
      (CQ (P3 (MIN 0)
              (MAX 0)
              (ARG (P2 (HAS-PROP V1) (PROP (FLIES)))))))))
and
((P1 (HAS-PROP (V1 <-- WINGED-HORSES)) (PROP (NOT-FLIES))))
I infer
((P3 (MIN 0)
     (MAX 0)
     (ARG (P2 (HAS-PROP (V1 <-- WINGED-HORSES))
              (PROP (FLIES)))))))
```

A contradiction was detected within context DEFAULT-DEFAULTCT.

The contradiction involves the newly derived node:

```
   (M13! (MIN 0)
         (MAX 0)
         (ARG (M4! (HAS-PROP (WINGED-HORSES))(PROP (FLIES)))))
```

and the previously existing node:

```
   (M4! (HAS-PROP (WINGED-HORSES)) (PROP (FLIES)))
```

In order to make the context consistent you must delete at least

one hypothesis from the following set of hypotheses:
   (M3! M4! M5! M8!)

At this point we get into an interactive package that enables the removal of hypotheses. In this example we remove hypothesis M5!. Afterwards the inference proceeds, returning the following nodes:

```
(M17! (MIN 0) (MAX 0) (ARG (M16 (HAS-PROP TORNADO) (PROP FLIES)))
      (DER ((ASSERTIONS (M2! M3! M8!))
              (RESTRICTION ((M4! M5))) (NAMED NIL))))

(M19! (MIN 0) (MAX 0) (ARG (M18 (HAS-PROP HORSES) (PROP FLIES)))
      (DER ((ASSERTIONS (M3! M8!))
              (RESTRICTION ((M4! M5))) (NAMED NIL))))

(M4! (HAS-PROP WINGED-HORSES) (PROP FLIES)
      (DER ((ASSERTIONS (M4!))
              (RESTRICTION ((M3! M5 M8!))) (NAMED NIL)))
      (HYP ((ASSERTIONS (M4!))
              (RESTRICTION ((M3! M5 M8!))) (NAMED NIL))))

(M9! (HAS-PROP PEGASUS) (PROP FLIES)
      (DER ((ASSERTIONS (M4! M7!))
              (RESTRICTION ((M3! M5 M8!))) (NAMED NIL))))
```

8 Conclusion

We discussed path-based inference in SNePS 2.1. The bulk of the work corresponded to the study of how to propagate dependencies among the propositions involved in the deduction so that the resulting propositions have adequate support. The work reported here was fully implemented and incorporated in SNePS 2.1.

9 Acknowledgements

This work was partially supported by Junta Nacional de Investigação Científica e Tecnológica (JNICT), under Grant 87-107 and by the Instituto Nacional de Investigação Científica.

10 References

Cravo M.R. and Martins J.P., "Path-Based Inference in SNeBR", in *Proc. EPIA 89*, Martins and Morgado (eds.), Heidelberg, W. Germany: Springer-Verlag, pp.97-106, 1989.

Martins J.P. and Shapiro S.C., "A Model for Belief Revision", *Journal of Artificial Intelligence*, vol. 35, N. 1, pp. 25-79, May 1988.

Shapiro S.C., "Path-Based and Node-Based Inference in Semantic Networks", *Theoretical Issues in Natural Language Processing 2*, pp. 219-225, 1978.

Shapiro S.C., "Cables and Path-Based Inference in Propositional Semantic Networks", DRAFT, August 1989a.

Shapiro S.C., *Personal Communication*, 1989b.

Shapiro S.C. and Rapaport W.J., "SNePS Considered as a Fully Intensional Propositional Semantic Network", in *The Knowledge Frontier: Essays in the Representation of Knowledge*, Cercone and McCalla (eds.), New York, N.Y." Springer Verlag, pp. 262-315, 1987.

Shapiro S.C. et. al., SNePS-2 User's Manual, Buffalo, N.Y.: Department of Computer Science, State University of New York at Buffalo, 1989.

Srihari R., "Combining Path-Based and Node-Based Inference in SNePS", Technical Report 183, Buffalo, N.Y.: Department of Computer Science, State University of New York at Buffalo, 1981.

Expanding SNePS Capabilities with LORE

Nuno J. Mamede
njm@inesc.inesc.pt

João P. Martins
ist_1416@ptifm.bitnet

Instituto Superior Técnico
Technical University of Lisbon
Av. Rovisco Pais
1000 Lisboa, Portugal

Abstract

We briefly describe LORE, a logic with four values, the traditional truth values T and F, and two "Unknown" values, allowing to differentiate between knowing that nothing is known, and not knowing (with the available resources) whether it is known. A computer system based on LORE has the capability to remember all the paths followed during an attempt to answer a question. For each path, it records the used hypotheses (the hypotheses that constitute the path), the missing hypotheses (when the path did not lead to an answer), and why they were assumed missing. A number of examples of the use of LORE are discussed, and it is shown that SNePS capabilities can be expanded if LORE is accepted as the logic underlying its inferences.

1 Introduction

Artificial Intelligence is interested in the development of intelligent Question-Answering systems able to perform Common Sense Reasoning. In this kind of systems one is engaged in a sort of "perpetual proof" during which propositions are told to the system, and the system's goal is to answer questions from a user. We think that the inadequacy of the existing systems, whenever used in real life situations, is partly due to assuming resources are infinite, and to their inability to supply the reasons that prevented an answer to be found. We are going to look more closely at each of these weaknesses.

Computers like *"... people are resource-bounded: they lack the computational resources to deduce all the logical consequences of their knowledge (we still don't know whether Fermat's last theorem is true)"* [Fagin and Halpern 87, pp. 40–41]. An ideal reasoner, with infinite computational power, is not appropriate for modeling human reasoning with limited capabilities. One slant on this problem which Hintikka named the local omniscience problem, lies in the assumption that agents know all valid formulas, and that their knowledge is closed under implication [Hintikka 75].

Some researchers have addressed the omniscience problem. The computational approach proposed by McKay, associates resources with each question [McKay 81]. This permits controlling the maximum computational effort that can be spent in answering a question. If wanted, it is possible to resume the computation with the addition of more resources. But the decision to give more resources is based on the user's intuition, since the inference system does not report either the paths it was following or where the computation was suspended.

Resources can be defined as something that is consumed by an inference system when it is trying to answer a question. McKay, for example, has proposed the operation of matching a pattern with the knowledge base as a resource unit [McKay 81], and Bobrow and Winograd have suggested the depth of search as a criterion to limit the number of inferences that can be made [Bobrow and Winograd 77].

It is also well known that for most question-answering systems, nothing is returned when a definite answer cannot be produced. This incapability is a burden on the user: is a piece of information missing? Was a piece of information mistyped? What is necessary to assume in order to get an answer? The few exceptions known are the MDS system [Srinivasan 76] and the KRL framework: *"In case in which the processing so far has not produced a definite answer , the matcher should be able to return specific details in addition to the result of 'don't know yet'. ... As the current version, only the 'hooks' for calling these mechanisms exist, and no details have been filled in."* [Bobrow and Winograd 77, p. 26].

Our proposal consists of combining the resources approach with the capability to inform the user about paths that have been followed and the impediments, if any, that have already been found for each of them. The possible impediments are of two kinds: either some knowledge is absent from the knowledge base or the resources are insufficient. These two situations are differentiated whenever results are reported to the user. We also inform the user whenever the absent knowledge, if introduced in the knowledge base, contradicts an existing proposition.

We present a four-valued logic, named LORE (from Logic and Resources), developed to deal with the problem of having limited resources. LORE is specially suitable as a tool for modeling intelligent agents with the ability to perform hypothetical reasoning, abductive reasoning, learning, reasoning about its own knowledge, and planning.

LORE is introduced in Section 2: we present the four truth values, introduce the connectives, describe the objects the logic deals with, the conditional supported wffs, and finally, make a brief reference to the inference rules. (In this paper this part is abbreviated; see [Mamede, Pinto-Ferreira and Martins 89] [Mamede and Martins 90] for a filling out.) Section 3 is devoted to presenting examples of the use of LORE and to show how SNePS capabilities can be expanded.

2   The LORE Logic

2.1   The Four Values

If someone is asked *"Do you know if Tina's phone number is 67543 ?"*, four possible answers can be expected:

1. *Yes, it is*;

2. *No, it isn't. The correct number is 67544*;

3. *I'm sorry, I don't know. By the way, who's Tina?*;

4. *I'm sorry but I don't know if I have it.*[1] *But, if you want I can look it up.*

The values of our logic are based on the above expected states of knowledge, which are epistemological states. The values of our many-valued logic are intended as epistemic, rather than ontic, in character.[2] Let us give them names:

KT (Known True): know it has been told so (with the available knowledge and the available resources);

KF (Known False): know it has been denied (with the available knowledge and the available resources);

KN (Known Neither): know it has been told nothing. It has not been told it and neither it has been denied (with the available knowledge and the available resources);

U (Unknown): don't know if it has either been told, or has been denied because we did not look for (there were no resources available).

The values KN and U represent two different states of knowledge, the first is a "state of knowledge" and the second is a "state of ignorance". The KN value means it is *known that it is unknown*, and the U value means it is *not known if it is either known or not known*.

Ackermann argues that the main motivation for considering many-valued logics is to sanction fewer arguments as valid than do standard logics [Ackermann 67, p. 43]. However this is not our intention, *our motivation is to determine the conditions that must be satisfied in order to sanction failed arguments*.

Our logic only enables to express explicitly that a proposition is either Known True or Known False, and implicitly that a proposition is Known Neither, not telling that it is either Known True or Known False. The available resources determine which propositions are Unknown. The vocabulary available is the same as in the classical logic.

2.2 The connectives NOT, AND, and OR

Tables 1a, b and c present the truth tables of the NOT, AND and OR connectives. Note that the three tables preserve many properties of the classical two-valued connectives.

Table 1b says that if one of the conjuncts is KN and the other is U then the conjunction is U, reflecting the state of uncertainty due to the conjunct with value U. If, for example, the conjunct with value U becomes (later on) KF, then the conjunction becomes (later on) KF too, and the state of uncertainty is removed. This same justification can be used for the disjunction.

---

[1] This is distinct from "I'm sorry but I don't remember", which means one is conscious of knowing the phone number but in this precise moment it is not possible to remember it.

[2] The former has to do with a person's knowledge or belief about a truth value, while the latter has to do with the truth value independently of anyone's knowledge of it.

¬	
KT	KF
KF	KT
KN	KN
U	U

a) NOT

∧	KT	KF	KN	U
KT	KT	KF	KN	U
KF	KF	KF	KF	KF
KN	KN	KF	KN	U
U	U	KF	U	U

b) AND

∨	KT	KF	KN	U
KT	KT	KT	KT	KT
KF	KT	KF	KN	U
KN	KT	KN	KN	U
U	KT	U	U	U

c) OR

Table 1: Truth tables for the NOT, AND and OR connectives

The semantics for the logic involving the three connectives is defined as usual. Given an arbitrary set-up s, which is a mapping of atomic formulas into the set {KT, KF, KN, U}, we can extend a mapping of all formulas into the set {KT, KF, KN, U} in the standard inductive way:

$$s(A \land B) = s(A) \land s(B)$$
$$s(A \lor B) = s(A) \lor s(B)$$
$$s(\neg B) = \neg s(B)$$

This tells what the value of a formula A is: the value of the formula A in s, i.e., $s(A)$. For more about this subject see [Mamede and Martins 90].

2.3 Entailment and Inference

For our purposes, and we are thinking of a Question-Answering system able to perform Common Sense Reasoning, the best interpretation of "A entails B" or "B follows logically from A" is that A is relevant to B. With "relevant" we mean that there must be some connection of meaning between them, i.e., A can be used to derive B [Anderson and Belnap 75].

We do not present a full semantics for entailment, but rather discuss it informally. For some authors, $A \rightarrow B$ means that the inference from A to B is valid in all truth values, so it can only be True or False [Belnap 77] [Driankov 88]. Due to the semantics of our truth values we want $A \rightarrow B$ to vary into the set {KT, KF, KN, U}. So, we define the function σ, that gives the value of $A \rightarrow B$:

$$\sigma(A \rightarrow B) = \begin{cases} \text{KT,} & \text{if there exists a proof of } B \text{ from } A \\ \text{KF,} & \text{if there exists a proof of } \neg B \text{ from } A \text{ and } A \text{ is KT} \\ \text{U,} & \text{if there exists a proof of } B \text{ from } A \text{ but conditionally to some premise with value U} \\ \text{KN,} & \text{otherwise}^3 \end{cases}$$

Entailment is used to generate implicit knowledge from what is explicitly known. The rule of Modus Ponens allows the derivation of B in the presence of A and $A \rightarrow B$, and the truth value of B is obtained as a function, named ModusP, of the truth-values of A and $A \rightarrow B$, Table 2a. The rule of Modus Tollens enables the derivation of $\neg A$ in the presence of $\neg B$ and $A \rightarrow B$, and the truth value of $\neg A$ is obtained as a function, called ModusT, of the truth-values of $\neg B$ and $A \rightarrow B$, Table 2b.

---

[3]Either there does not exist a proof of B from A, or a proof of $\neg B$ from A when A is KT, or there exists a proof of B from A but conditionally to premise(s) with value(s) KN, but not U.

B		A→B			
		KT	KF	KN	U
	KT	KT	KN	KN	U
A	KF	KN	KN	KN	KN
	KN	KN	KN	KN	U
	U	U	KN	U	U

a) Function ModusP

¬A		A→B			
		KT	KF	KN	U
	KT	KT	KN	KN	U
¬B	KF	KN	KN	KN	KN
	KN	KN	KN	KN	U
	U	U	KN	U	U

b) Function ModusT

Table 2: Definition of the functions ModusP and ModusT

Due to these two rules (Modus Ponens and Modus Tollens), a proposition can have different (proposed) values. Suppose the following propositions are KT: "A→C", "B→C", and "A". Since "A→C" and "A" are KT, it is possible to conclude that "C" is also KT. On the other hand, since "B→C" is KT, and assuming nothing is known about "B" it can be concluded "C" is KN. So, "C" has simultaneously the value KT and the value KN.

These values are related to the propositions that were used to determine them. This is a new way to look at the truth values, they are "special" values, and should be interpreted as possible values, or the value of the proposition if a different value is not "proposed" too. For example, "C" is KT, if we only consider the propositions "A→C" and "A", and is KN, if we only consider propositions "B→C" and "B" (which is KN). This is very important in AI, where the notion of "Universal Truth" does not hold, but instead, there are knowledge bases with propositions from where new propositions can be derived.

We can think of a function Υ that decides which is the value of a proposition when *different* values have been "proposed":

$$\Upsilon(v_1 \ldots v_n) = \begin{cases} KT, & \text{if } \exists_{1 \leq i \leq n} \ v_i = KT \\ KF, & \text{if } \exists_{1 \leq i \leq n} \ v_i = KF \\ KN, & \text{if } \forall_{1 \leq i \leq n} \ v_i = KN \\ U, & \text{otherwise} \end{cases}$$

This function enables a proposition being simultaneously KT and KF, which should be interpreted, as usual, as a contradiction. However, if follows that propositions with value either KN or U are not contradictory with any other proposition. This definition has the advantage of considering the values correspondent to the lack of information (KN and U) weaker than the other values (KT and KF). Some of the entailment rules are formally described in Section 2.5.

2.4 Conditional Supported wffs

The SWM system [Martins 83] [Martins and Shapiro 88], which we took as the starting point for developing our logic, deals with objects called *supported wffs*. A supported wff consists of a wff and an associated triple, its *support*, containing an *origin tag*, an *origin set*, and a *restriction set*. The *origin set*, references every hypothesis used in the derivation of its wff. The *restriction set* contains information about which sets unioned with the wff's origin set produce an inconsistent set, and the *origin tag* is an identifier used to know whether a given wff was introduced as a hypothesis (*hyp*) or was derived from other wffs (*der* or *ext*[4]).

The SWM's support is used to record the hypotheses used in the derivation of a wff. Since we also want to register the hypotheses that, if present, enable the derivation of a wff, we have to extend it. An extended support is used to record the hypotheses needed to derive a wff where some of them may not be available at the moment. This new support is called *conditional support*, and the resulting supported wffs are called *conditional supported wffs*. As in the SWM system, multiple derivations of the same wff correspond to different conditional supported wffs.

In a system with limited resources there are two possible reasons to justify the absence of a wff, either it cannot be derived, or there are not enough resources. This, and the information about whatever absent hypothesis is contradictory with any other wff is stored in the conditional support. A conditional supported wff consists of a wff and an associated quintuplet containing an *origin tag* (OT), an *origin set* (OS), a *neither set* (NS), an *unknown set* (US) and a *contradictory set* (CS). We write $\langle A, \tau, \alpha, [\sigma, \delta, \beta]\rangle$ to denote that A is a wff with OT τ, OS α, NS σ, US δ and CS β.

The OS, NS, US and CS are sets of hypotheses, and the OT has exactly the same interpretation as in SWM. The union of the four sets of a conditional supported wff, determines exactly which hypotheses were used to derive the wff: the OS contains the hypotheses that already exist; the NS contains the hypotheses that do not exist and the equivalent propositions could not be derived; the US contains the hypotheses that are not possible to know if they exist, or if they can be derived since the available resources are insufficient; and the CS contains the hypotheses that are contradictory with another wff.[5]

A conditional supported wff with empty NS, US, and CS must be interpreted in the same way as SWM's supported wffs: the wff is a hypothesis or has been successfully deduced. If at least one of these sets is not empty then the conditional supported wff can be interpreted as the derivation of the wff being conditional: if all the hypotheses of NS, US and CS were present then the wff would have been derived and the hypotheses used to derive it would be given by the union of OS, NS, US and CS. If the CS is not empty then a contradiction may be derived. This is a positive (optimistic) reading of a failure. All the sets that constitute a conditional support share the same kind of information: the hypotheses necessary to derive a wff.

The conditional support is a "mirror" of the truth-value of a conditional supported wff $\langle A, \tau, \alpha, [\sigma, \delta, \beta]\rangle$:

- if σ, δ and β are empty sets then A has the truth value KT;
- if either σ or β are not empty sets but δ is, then A has the truth value KN;
- If δ is not an empty set then A has the truth value U.

We say that a wff A has the value KF when the conditional supported wff $\langle \neg A, \tau, \alpha, [-, -, -]\rangle$[6] is

---

[4]*ext* identifies special wffs whose origin set was extended and has to be treated specially in order to avoid the introduction of irrelevancies. A detailed discussion of this issue can be found in [Martins and Shapiro 88, p.37].

[5]It is not necessary for the contradictory wff to be a hypothesis.

[6]A dash is used to represent the empty set {}.

present in the knowledge base.[7]

2.5 Some Inference Rules

Most of LORE's inference rules are generalizations of the SWM's inference rules. Here, we only present some of the inference rules, the full set is described in [Mamede and Martins 90]:

Hypothesis (Hyp) This rule allows us to add new information to the knowledge base: for any wff A, we may add the conditional supported wff $\langle A, hyp, \{A\}, [-, -, -]\rangle$ to the knowledge base, provided that A has not already been introduced as a hypothesis.

Neither (Neither) This rule allows the introduction of knowledge that is both absent and not derivable: for any wff A, we may add the conditional supported wff $\langle A, hyp, -, [\{A\}, -, -]\rangle$ to the knowledge base, provided that that A has not already been introduced as a hypothesis.

Unknown (Unkn) This rule enables the introduction of wffs when there are no available resources to know if they have either been introduced as hypotheses, or can be derived: for any wff A, we may add the conditional supported wff $\langle A, hyp, -, [-, \{A\}, -]\rangle$ to the knowledge base.

Implication Introduction ($\rightarrow$I)

$\rightarrow$I$_1$ This rule is a generalization of the traditional relevant rule to introduce entailments:

>From $\langle B, der, o, [n, u, c]\rangle$ and any hypothesis[8] $H \in (o \cup n \cup u \cup c)$, infer $\langle H \rightarrow B, der, o - \{H\}, [n - \{H\}, u - \{H\}, c - \{H\}]\rangle$.

Notice that every hypothesis in the OS, NS, US or CS of B *is necessary* in its derivation, and thus it implies B under the assumption of the remaining hypotheses. The hypothesis H is subtracted to all hypotheses sets, but it is present in only one of the sets.

$\rightarrow$I$_2$ This rule enables the introduction of the negation of an entailment:

>From $\langle \neg B, der, o_1, [n_1, u_1, c_1]\rangle$, any hypothesis $H \in (o_1 \cup n_1 \cup u_1 \cup c_1)$ and $\langle \neg H, t, o_2, [-, -, -]\rangle$ infer $\langle \neg(H \rightarrow B), \Lambda(t, t)[9], o_1 \cup o_2 - \{H\}, [n - \{H\}, u - \{H\}, c - \{H\}]\rangle$.

Modus Ponens—Implication Elimination (MP)

MP$_1$ This rule is a generalization of the SWM's rule of Modus Ponens:

>From $\langle A, t_1, o_1, [n_1, u_1, c_1]\rangle$, $\langle A \rightarrow B, t_2, o_2, [n_2, u_2, c_2]\rangle$, infer $\langle B, \Lambda(t_1, t_2), o_1 \cup o_2, [n_1 \cup n_2, u_1 \cup u_2, c_1 \cup c_2]\rangle$.

MP$_2$ This rule enables the introduction of the antecedent of the entailment as a hypothesis, when it is contradictory with another wff present in the knowledge base:

From $\langle \neg A, t_1, o_1, [-, -, -]\rangle$, $\langle A \rightarrow B, t_2, o_2, [n_2, u_2, c_2]\rangle$, infer $\langle B, \Lambda(t_1, t_2), o_2, [n_2, u_2, c_2 \cup \{A\}]\rangle$.

---

[7]The set of all conditional supported wffs.

[8]A conditional supported wff whose OT is *hyp*.

[9]The Λ function computes the OT of a supported wff resulting from the application of the rules of inference, (see [Mamede, Pinto-Ferreira and Martins 89]).

3   Expanding SNePS Capabilities

Since SWM is the logic that underlies SNePS [Shapiro 79] [Shapiro et al. 89], and SWM has been taken as the starting point for developing LORE, we will address the current limitations of SNePS and how SNePS$_{LORE}$[10] overcomes them, to stand out LORE's improvements.

We are going to show some of the advantages of substituting SWM for LORE, as the underlying logic in SNePS. The following examples exhibit LORE's potentialities: (i) reporting the reasons that prevented answering a question; (ii) avoiding the problems currently existing with hypothetical reasoning when a contradiction can be derived as a consequence of raising a new hypothesis; (iii) reporting negative answers when trying to prove an entailment or a conjunction; (iv) performing abductive reasoning; (v) learning with inference.

3.1   More Friendly

Whenever SNePS is asked to answer a question, and no answer is found, nothing is reported but an "absolute silence". Contrariwise, SNePS$_{LORE}$ has the ability to supply the reasons that prevented the question to be answered, facilitating the development of friendly user interfaces.

Suppose that our knowledge base contains the following conditional supported wffs:

$$\langle E{\rightarrow}A,\ hyp,\ \{E{\rightarrow}A\},\ [\text{-},\text{-},\text{-}]\rangle$$
$$\langle (B{\wedge}C){\rightarrow}A,\ hyp,\ \{(B{\wedge}C){\rightarrow}A\},\ [\text{-},\text{-},\text{-}]\rangle$$
$$\langle D{\rightarrow}C,\ hyp,\ \{D{\rightarrow}C\},\ [\text{-},\text{-},\text{-}]\rangle$$
$$\langle \neg E,\ hyp,\ \{\neg E\},\ [\text{-},\text{-},\text{-}]\rangle$$
$$\langle B,\ hyp,\ \{B\},\ [\text{-},\text{-},\text{-}]\rangle$$

If an attempt is made to derive A the Neither rule can be used, allowing the introduction of:

$$\langle D,\ hyp,\ \text{-},\ [\{D\},\ \text{-},\ \text{-}]\rangle$$

MP$_1$ and $\wedge$I rules sanction:

$$\langle C,\ der,\ \{D{\rightarrow}C\},\ [\{D\},\ \text{-},\ \text{-}]\rangle$$
$$\langle B{\wedge}C,\ ext,\ \{D{\rightarrow}C,B\},\ [\{D\},\ \text{-},\ \text{-}]\rangle$$

and finally, using (respectively) MP$_1$ and MP$_2$ rules:

$$\langle A,\ ext,\ \{(B{\wedge}C){\rightarrow}A,D{\rightarrow}C,B\},\ [\{D\},\ \text{-},\ \text{-}]\rangle$$
$$\langle A,\ der,\ \{E{\rightarrow}A\},\ [\text{-},\text{-},\{E\}]\rangle$$

The last two wffs can have the following interpretation (reading): *There are two different possibilities to derive A: either we accept D (although nothing is known about it) or, we accept E which is contradictory with another existing proposition.*

3.2   Hypothetical Reasoning

SNePS enables the proof of entailments, simulating subproofs by means of contexts and belief spaces: *"... to prove the entailment $A{\rightarrow}B$, it [SNePS] creates a new context by adding the hypothesis A to the current context (the context in which the entailment was asked to be proved) and tries to prove B within the Belief Space defined by this new context."* [Martins and Shapiro 86, p. 1037]

---

[10]A future version of SNePS, having LORE as the underlying logic.

Difficulties arrive whenever a contradiction is detected as a consequence of the addition, although temporary, of the new hypothesis: SNePS stops the computation to find out a culprit for the contradiction. SNePS does not have the capability to recognize that hypothetical reasoning is being performed. It could seem that the solution to this problem consists of recognizing the temporary hypothesis as the culprit, but it is inadequate by reason of not proving the entailment. SNePS cannot prove the entailment "$A{\rightarrow}C$", (unless the user chooses the option of continuing the reasoning within an inconsistent set of hypotheses), in any of the following situations:

$$A{\rightarrow}B \qquad\qquad A{\rightarrow}B \qquad\qquad A{\rightarrow}B$$
$$B{\rightarrow}C \qquad\qquad B{\rightarrow}C \qquad\qquad B{\rightarrow}C$$
$$\neg A \qquad\qquad\quad \neg B \qquad\qquad\quad \neg C$$
$$A{\rightarrow}C? \qquad\qquad A{\rightarrow}C? \qquad\qquad A{\rightarrow}C?$$

To prove entailments, SNePS$_{\text{LORE}}$ does not have to raise new hypotheses. Additionally, conditional supported wffs whose union of its NS, US and CS is not an empty set, are not considered as contradictory with any other conditional supported wff (see function Υ defined on Section 2.3). So, the problem pointed out to SNePS does not occur in SNePS$_{\text{LORE}}$. For example, if we have:

$$\langle A{\rightarrow}B, \, hyp, \, \{A{\rightarrow}B\}, \, [\text{-}, \text{-}, \text{-}]\rangle$$
$$\langle B{\rightarrow}C, \, hyp, \, \{B{\rightarrow}C\}, \, [\text{-}, \text{-}, \text{-}]\rangle$$
$$\langle \neg A, \, hyp, \, \{\neg A\}, \, [\text{-}, \text{-}, \text{-}]\rangle$$

To prove the entailment $A{\rightarrow}C$ it is enough to derive C and verify if A has been used. The rule of MP$_2$ sanctions:

$$\langle B, \, der, \, \{A{\rightarrow}B\}, \, [\text{-}, \text{-}, \{A\}]\rangle$$
$$\langle C, \, der, \, \{A{\rightarrow}B, B{\rightarrow}C\}, \, [\text{-}, \text{-}, \{A\}]\rangle$$

finally, the $\rightarrow$I rule gives:

$$\langle A{\rightarrow}C, \, der, \, \{A{\rightarrow}B, B{\rightarrow}C\}, \, [\text{-}, \text{-}, \text{-}]\rangle$$

and no contradictory conditional supported wffs have either been added to the knowledge base or derived.

3.3 Reporting "Negation"

SNePS never reports a negative answer whenever trying to prove an entailment or a conjunction, (even when the available information and the common sense suggest it), because there is no SWM rule to sanction the deduction. For example, SNePS remains silent when asked to prove the entailment "$A{\rightarrow}C$" in the following situation:

$$A$$
$$A{\rightarrow}B$$
$$B{\rightarrow}(\neg C)$$
$$A{\rightarrow}C?$$

Since LORE, on the contrary, has the above missing inference rules, SNePS$_{\text{LORE}}$ has the capability to give negative answers whenever trying to prove entailments or disjunctions. The above example can be represented by the following conditional supported wffs:

$$\langle A, hyp, \{A\}, [-, -, -]\rangle$$
$$\langle A {\rightarrow} B, hyp, \{A {\rightarrow} B\}, [-, -, -]\rangle$$
$$\langle B {\rightarrow} (\neg C), hyp, \{B {\rightarrow} (\neg C)\}, [-, -, -]\rangle$$

the rule of MP$_1$ validates the deduction of:

$$\langle B, der, \{A, A {\rightarrow} B\}, [-, -, -]\rangle$$
$$\langle \neg C, der, \{A, A {\rightarrow} B, B {\rightarrow} (\neg C)\}, [-, -, -]\rangle$$

finally, the rule of $\rightarrow$I$_2$ enables the derivation of:

$$\langle \neg(A {\rightarrow} C), der, \{A, A {\rightarrow} B, B {\rightarrow} (\neg C)\}, [-, -, -]\rangle$$

3.4   Abduction

Abductive reasoning is an attempt to explain an observed phenomenon, i.e., finding hypotheses, not incompatible with other knowledge, from which the conclusion follows deductively [Holland et al. 86] [Reichgelt 87] [Reiter and de Kleer 87].

SNePS$_{LORE}$ enables the search for explanatory hypotheses, constrained by the current contents of the knowledge base. The found hypotheses are recorded in the CS, NS or US of the conditional support. The following example is from [Reiter and de Kleer 87, p. 184]:

$$(P {\wedge} Q {\wedge} R) {\rightarrow} G$$
$$(\neg P {\wedge} Q) {\rightarrow} G$$
$$(\neg Q {\wedge} R) {\rightarrow} G$$

Assuming no other information is available, an intelligent reasoner can conclude that G has three trivial abductive explanations:

$$P {\wedge} Q {\wedge} R \quad \vee \quad \neg P {\wedge} Q \quad \vee \quad \neg Q {\wedge} R$$

which can be simplified:

$$\neg P {\wedge} Q \quad \vee \quad R$$

SNePS$_{LORE}$ can compute abductive explanations. Let's consider the last example:

$$\langle (P {\wedge} Q {\wedge} R) {\rightarrow} G, hyp, \{(P {\wedge} Q {\wedge} R) {\rightarrow} G\}, [-, -, -]\rangle$$
$$\langle (\neg P {\wedge} Q) {\rightarrow} G, hyp, \{(\neg P {\wedge} Q) {\rightarrow} G\}, [-, -, -]\rangle$$
$$\langle (\neg Q {\wedge} R) {\rightarrow} G, hyp, \{(\neg Q {\wedge} R) {\rightarrow} G\}, [-, -, -]\rangle$$

LORE rules (Neither, $\wedge$I and MP$_1$) enable the following derivations:

$$\langle G, ext, (P {\wedge} Q {\wedge} R) {\rightarrow} G, [\{P, Q, R\}, -, -]\rangle$$
$$\langle G, ext, \{(\neg P {\wedge} Q) {\rightarrow} G\}, [\{\neg P, Q\}, -, -]\rangle$$
$$\langle G, ext, \{(\neg Q {\wedge} R) {\rightarrow} G\}, [\{\neg Q, R\}, -, -]\rangle$$

and the conjunction of all the hypotheses present in the NS, US and CS of each of these conditional supported wffs gives one of the trivial explanations:

$$P {\wedge} Q {\wedge} R \qquad \neg P {\wedge} Q \qquad \neg Q {\wedge} R$$

These explanations are not the simplest possible ones, however its computation can be determined by an appropriate algorithm [Slagle, Chang and Lee 69] [Minicozzi and Reiter 72].

3.5 Learning with Reasoning

We humans, do not reason with what we don't have the conscience of not knowing, but when aware of our ignorance, we can use it (the ignorance) in our speculations. It is usual to accept that someone conscious of his ignorance surpasses, in power of reasoning, those not conscious.

Since SNePS$_{LORE}$ only enables to express implicitly that a proposition is not known (not telling that it is either Known True or Known False), before starting to reason, the knowledge base reflects a complete state of ignorance of its limitations. LORE's inference rules have the power of changing implicit into explicit ignorance, which gives SNePS$_{LORE}$ the ability to learn with experience, i.e., augment its capabilities with the process of answering questions.

As an example, suppose that SNePS$_{LORE}$'s knowledge base only has the following conditional supported wffs:

$$\langle B{\rightarrow}A, hyp, \{B{\rightarrow}A\}, [\text{-}, \text{-}, \text{-}]\rangle$$
$$\langle D{\rightarrow}C, hyp, \{D{\rightarrow}C\}, [\text{-}, \text{-}, \text{-}]\rangle$$

if asked to prove the entailment $D{\rightarrow}A$, SNePS$_{LORE}$ returns:

$$\langle D{\rightarrow}A, hyp, \text{-}, [\{D{\rightarrow}A\}, \text{-}, \text{-}]\rangle$$

which should be understood as nothing is known about it.

Now, suppose SNePS$_{LORE}$ is asked to prove the entailment $C{\rightarrow}B$ (the "intelligent" question). Since, nothing is known about this entailment, the answer is:

$$\langle C{\rightarrow}B, hyp, \text{-}, [\{C{\rightarrow}B\}, \text{-}, \text{-}]\rangle$$

and SNePS$_{LORE}$ becomes conscious of not knowing $C{\rightarrow}B$. Now if asked, once more, to prove the entailment $D{\rightarrow}A$ the Neither and MP$_1$ rules enable the derivation of:

$$\langle D, hyp, \text{-}, [\{D\}, \text{-}, \text{-}]\rangle$$
$$\langle C, der, \{D{\rightarrow}C\}, [\{D\}, \text{-}, \text{-}]\rangle$$
$$\langle B, der, \{D{\rightarrow}C\}, [\{C{\rightarrow}B, D\}, \text{-}, \text{-}]\rangle$$
$$\langle A, der, \{D{\rightarrow}C, B{\rightarrow}A\}, [\{C{\rightarrow}B, D, A\}, \text{-}, \text{-}]\rangle$$

and finally the rule of $\rightarrow$I sanctions:

$$\langle D{\rightarrow}A, der, \{D{\rightarrow}C, B{\rightarrow}A\}, [\{C{\rightarrow}B, D\}, \text{-}, \text{-}]\rangle$$

SNePS$_{LORE}$ was more competent when asked the second time to prove the entailment $D{\rightarrow}A$ because it became aware of its limitations.

4 Conclusion

The main objective of this work is to provide a mechanism that will properly explore the introduction of resources into inference systems. It is our opinion that an inference system based on our concepts will provide the information necessary to perform a wide sort of tasks, such as planning, abduction, to carry out hypothetical reasoning, and reasoning about its own knowledge.

We presented a logic with four values: Known True, Known False, Known Neither and Unknown. The basic justification for the introduction of the two new values was the need to distinguish between "not finding an answer but resources were not a problem" and "not finding an answer but with more resources perhaps an answer could be found". The semantics of NOT, AND, and OR were presented, and entailment was treated informally. A deduction system based on this logic was introduced, which has the capability to record the hypotheses necessary to derive a given wff, where some of them may not be available.

We have shown some of the advantages of substituting SWM for LORE, as the underlying system of logic in SNePS. Examples were used to exhibit LORE's potentialities, namely, to perform hypothetical reasoning, abductive reasoning, and to learn with the experience of answering questions. We also proved the utility of LORE as a tool in the development of friendly interfaces. We also think LORE is an appropriate tool to perform the planning of inference and to perform default reasoning.

The detection and handling of contradictions, the existence of inference rules capable of updating the conditional supports when new hypotheses are introduced, and the handling of the "non-standard connectives" [Shapiro 79] constitute work in progress.

Acknowledgement

All this research is a consequence of a suggestion made by Carlos Pinto-Ferreira, during one of the many meetings we hold regularly. Many thanks to John Kearns, Bill Rapaport, and Stuart Shapiro, for their general discussions while the research was in progress.

This work was partially supported by Fundação Luso Americana para o Desenvolvimento (FLAD), by Instituto de Engenharia de Sistemas e Computadores (INESC), and by Grant 87-107 of Junta Nacional de Investigação Científica e Tecnológica (JNICT).

References

[Ackermann 67] Ackermann, R., *An Introduction to Many-Valued Logics*, (Dover Publications Inc., New York, 1967).

[Anderson and Belnap 75] Anderson, A. and Belnap, N., *Entailment: The Logic of Relevance and Necessity* 1, (Princeton University Press, Princeton, NJ, 1975).

[Belnap 77] Belnap, N., A Useful Four-Valued Logic, in: G. Epstein and J.M. Dunn (Eds.), *Modern Uses of Multiple-Valued Logic*, (Reidel, Dordrecht, The Netherlands, 1977).

[Bobrow and Winograd 77] Bobrow, D. and Winograd, T., An Overview of KRL, a Knowledge Representation Language, *Cognitive Science* 1 (1) (1977) 3–46.

[Donlond 82] Donlon, G., *Using Resource Limited Inference in SNePS*, SNeRG Technical Note 10, Department of Computer Science, State University of New York at Buffalo, Buffalo, NY, 1982.

[Driankov 88] Driankov, D., Towards a Many-Valued Logic of Quantified Belief, Ph.D. Dissertation, Thesis 192, Department of Computer and Information Science, Linköping University, Linköping, Sweden, 1988.

[Fagin and Halpern 87] Fagin, R. and Halpern, J., Belief, Awareness, and Limited Reasoning, *Artificial Intelligence* 34 (1) (1987) 39–76.

[Hintikka 75] Hintikka, J., Impossible Possible Worlds Vindicated, *J. Philosophical Logic* 4 (1975) 475–484.

[Holland et al. 86] Holland, J., Holyoak, K., Nisbett, R. and Thagard, P., *Induction: Processes of Inference, Learning, and Discovery*, (MIT Press, Cambridge, Massachusetts, 1986).

[Mamede, Pinto-Ferreira and Martins 89] Mamede, N., Pinto-Ferreira, C. and Martins, J., Reasoning with the Unknown, in: Martins and Morgado (Eds.), *Proc. 4th Portuguese Conference on Artificial Intelligence, Lecture Notes in Artificial Intelligence 390*, (Springer-Verlag, Berlin, 1989) 85–96.

[Mamede and Martins 90] Mamede, N. and Martins, J., *Bringing Resources into Logic*, (submitted for publication).

[Martins 83] Martins, J., *Reasoning in Multiple Belief Spaces*, Ph.D. Dissertation, Technical Report 203, Department of Computer Science, State University of New York at Buffalo, Buffalo, NY, 1983.

[Martins and Shapiro 86] Martins, J. and Shapiro, S., Hypothetical Reasoning, in: Sriram and Adey (Eds.), *Applications of Artificial Intelligence in Engineering Problems: Proceedings of the First International Conference*, (Springer-Verlag, Berlin, West Germany, 1986) 1029–1042.

[Martins and Shapiro 88] Martins, J. and Shapiro, S., A Model for Belief Revision, *Artificial Intelligence* **35** (1) (1988) 25–79.

[McKay 81] McKay, D., *Monitors: Structuring Control Information*, Thesis Proposal, Department of Computer Science, State University of New York at Buffalo, Buffalo, NY, 1981.

[Minicozzi and Reiter 72] Minicozzi, E. and Reiter, R., A Note on Linear Resolution Strategies in Consequence-Finding, *Artificial Intelligence* **3** (1–4) (1972) 175–180.

[Reichgelt 87] Reichgelt, H., A Review of McDermott's "Critique of Pure Reason", *The European Journal on Artificial Intelligence* **0** (1) (1987) 39–42.

[Reiter and de Kleer 87] Reiter R., and de Kleer, J., Foundations of Assumption-Based Truth Maintenance Systems: Preliminary Report, in: *Proceedings AAAI-87*, Seattle, Washington (1987) 183–188.

[Shapiro 79] Shapiro, S., The SNePS Semantic Network Processing System, in: Findler (Ed.), *Associative Networks: The Representation and Use of Knowledge by Computers*, (Academic Press, New York, 1979) 179–203.

[Shapiro 89] Shapiro, S., Personal Communication, 1989.

[Shapiro et al. 89] Shapiro, S. and The SNePS Implementation Group, *SNePS-2 User's Manual*, Department of Computer Science, State University of New York at Buffalo, Buffalo, NY, 1989.

[Slagle, Chang and Lee 69] Slagle, J., Chang, C. and Lee, R., Completeness Theorems for Semantic Resolution in Consequence-Finding in: *Proceedings IJCAI-69*, Washington, D.C., (1969) 281-285.

[Srinivasan 76] Srinivasan, C., The Architecture of Coherent Information Systems, *IEEE Transactions on Computers* **C-25** (4) (1976) 390–402.

Order Dependence of Declarative Knowledge Representation

James Geller

Department of Computer and Information Sciences

New Jersey Institute of Technology

Newark, NJ 07102

geller@mars.njit.edu

Abstract

It has been a widely accepted assumption among knowledge representation researchers that declarative knowledge representation is in some sense order independent. In this paper we will argue that there are a number of different possible senses of the term "order independent" and that one needs at least one type of order dependence to develop a cognitively valid knowledge representation system that takes knowledge acquisition into account.

We will distinguish between spatial, temporal, and conceptual order dependence. We argue that any system dealing with a changing knowledge base should maintain the conceptual order implied by the chronological order of the concepts it is acquiring. It will be shown for the SNePS (Semantic Network Processing System) system that order dependence can be incorporated without any changes to the theory or interpreter of the system.

1 Introduction

Many researchers in the AI community hold that one of the attractive features of declarative knowledge representation for natural language processing [1] is its order independence. For instance Pitrat [13] writes that

> Using declarative knowledge is beneficial because of its convenience and efficiency. . . . The components of the knowledge are independent, so we can remove, add, or modify them independently of each other.

The idea of order-independence of declarative knowledge goes a long way back. In "the paper that started it all" (according to Brachman & Levesque, [3]) McCarthy [12]states that

---

[1]Our main interest in knowledge representation is for natural language processing.

> The meaning of declaratives is much less dependent on their order than is the case
> with imperatives. This makes it easier to have afterthoughts.

The reader will notice that McCarthy's quote is much more conservative than Pitrat's. McCarthy does not make an absolute statement about the possibility to add or modify declarative structures independently from each other, only one that compares declarative structures to imperative ones.

One of the few exceptions to the order independence assumption has been presented by Shapiro and Maida [18]. In an elaborate argument, which we cannot reproduce here, the authors show that the semantic network structure representing a chain of natural language utterances might appear in two different formats, if extensionally identical objects are represented by intensionally different concepts.

In this paper we will distinguish between different meanings of the term "order independence" and present a few arguments why a cognitively valid model of declarative knowledge should *not* be order independent in one of these senses. We will show that such order dependencies occur in much simpler situations than the one described by Maida and Shapiro. We will also exhibit connections between our theory and Harnad's theory of "symbol grounding" [8]. Finally it will be pointed out that the SNePS [17, 19] system in its current implementation can deal with the changes that we are proposing.

2   Senses of Order Dependence

There are at least three different meanings that one can assign to the phrase "order independent."

1. It may mean that order independence denotes a strictly temporal phenomenon. Input to some system can be given in any desired temporal order, and the behavior of the system will not depend on this order.

2. Order independence could also mean that the knowledge base of the system is editable and one may add a new structure between any pair of existing structures. This type of independence is exhibited by systems like OPS-5 [4] and is a spatial phenomenon of the knowledge representation. The behavior of the system will be independent of this spatial order.

3. Finally, order independence could mean *conceptual order independence*. In this sense, more advanced (possibly abstract) concepts can be entered into a system, independently whether the simpler (probably concrete) concepts they are relying on are already known to the system or not. Note that although this sounds similar to temporal order independence, it is orthogonal to it, because it focuses on the acquisition behavior, not the "run time behavior" of a system.

We hold, that conceptual order independence precludes any cognitively valid system that can combine knowledge representation with knowledge acquisition.

3   Arguments for Conceptually Ordered Knowledge

The first observation to be made is that natural language and research in natural language processing are intimately connected with research in knowledge representation. Weischedel [22] reviews common issues of these two topics. With a few early exceptions like ELIZA [23] all major natural language processing systems incorporate some formalism of knowledge representation. On the other hand, the development of knowledge representation itself has received its major motivation by work in natural language processing.

If one takes a paragraph of English text and reorders the sentences in it, this will usually result in a severe reduction of understandability. Some part of this effect is due to anaphora that refer back to earlier sentences, but replacing them by the terms they refer to would not eliminate the problem. A paragraph is simply more than a set of sentences, as has been shown in research on paragraph sized text [9].

Given the ordering constraints in text and the intimate relation between text and knowledge it seems somewhat surprising that declarative knowledge representation should be completely order independent.

Our second argument is as follows. Looking at the logical structure of connected text or speech, one often finds sentences that define a new term. This is especially true in scientific, legal, and mathematical language. One would expect that the definition of a new term occurs before or shortly after its use. This constraint on language structure should be mirrored in the knowledge representation of the corresponding text. [2]

This dependence goes to the point that a knowledge representation system that attempts to be cognitively valid should be **permitted** to reject a sentence if it detects an abundance of undefined terms. After definition and use of a new term have been added to a knowledge base, the knowledge structures should reflect that one of these concepts relies on one or more of the others.

A third argument for order dependence of knowledge representations can be based on the knowledge acquisition behavior of children. Although every child experiences its own distinct development, there are certain stages common to them [5]. In the beginning one word statements abound, and only after some time children will form sentence-like structures. In their utterances concrete expressions will precede abstract ones.

It seems counterintuitive that we should assume that a child will understand the sentence "Lucy padded a yellow dog," if the child does not know what a dog is, and does not know what "padding" means. Even if it derives and stores some information from this sentence, it seems unlikely that its internal representation will be complete and identical to the one that we would attribute to an adult who is familiar with the concepts of dog and padding.

Although we do not want to jump to any conclusions, it seems that one needs to have a certain selection of concrete knowledge before abstract knowledge can be built. Again, this means that one cannot add concrete and abstract knowledge in any random order, at least not during early

---

[2]Terry Nutter has pointed out to me that the teaching style of Russian mathematicians is diametrically opposed to this statement. They start with a theorem and develop all the necessary background for it. It seems that they must rely on some naive grounding of the used terms, and that they could not explain a theorem using artificial terms like xykryk. In any event, this phenomenon requires more study.

development.

So far we have looked at knowledge representation as a repository for natural language, knowledge representation as expressing the internal structure of paragraph sized pieces of text, and children's acquisition of knowledge structures.

For our fourth argument we will add the perspective of reasoning. Knowledge structures are not necessarily acquired, but in many cases they are derived from previous knowledge by the use of reasoning rules. If a structure A that is the premise for another structure B is withdrawn, it might become necessary to eliminate structure B also. This type of reasoning maintenance has been initiated by Doyle [6] and has led to the active field of research and development of truth maintenance systems (TMS). It demonstrates another example of knowledge structures for which an explicit order has to be maintained. While the previous three arguments involve problems with "independently adding" knowledge structures, this argument shows that one cannot "independently remove" knowledge structures. This stands in visible contrast to Pitrat's previously cited strong statement.

We will now present two more arguments that deal with adding knowledge. Lenat [11] presents several statements to the nature that one cannot learn something unless one almost knows it. He quotes personal communication with Porter saying that, "nothing new is learned except with respect to what's already known." We have developed a metaphor based on this statement.

Adding a single structure to a knowledge base seems like adding a piece to a jigsaw puzzle. This is an activity which is best done in an orderly fashion, starting at some corner, and growing along the edges, and finally into the middle. Staying with the same metaphor, one can start from different corners at the same time, or even grow small islands, but one cannot randomly plant pieces into free space and expect that they will grow together.

In our paradigm of conceptual ordering of knowledge structures that means that one cannot add a knowledge structure if it does not "touch" one or more already existing knowledge structures. In the context of a semantic network, touching means to "share a concept." One may create temporary "islands" but not too many of them, and they have to grow together at some point in time.

The last argument appeals to the (presumed) teaching experience of the reader. In introducing a new subject, one usually makes an assumption as a teacher that students know certain underlying facts. Often it turns out that this is not true for some students. By listening to a question a teacher can often derive what the missing link between the students knowledge and the teachers new item of information is. This indicates that some sort of ordering information is maintained between the structures of the subject which is sufficient to pin down a specific missing element.

On the other hand, it is easy to realize for a teacher if a student is at a knowledge level that is too low to bridge the existing gap with a simple explanation.

4 Arguments against Order Dependence

Our previous arguments raise a number of questions some of which we will address in this section.

4.1 Acquisition Versus Representation

The first question is whether we are confusing issues of knowledge acquisition with issues of knowledge representation. The definition of conceptual order dependence and most of the arguments given in favor of this order dependence make reference to the addition of knowledge to a knowledge base.

As mentioned in passing in a previous section we are mostly interested in knowledge representation for purposes of natural language processing. One can divide the tasks involved in natural language understanding into two different groups of subtasks, depending whether a parsed discourse introduces new concepts or not. If new concepts are introduced, then we would like to call this type of natural language processing *learning by being told.* [3]

Obviously, learning by being told involves the acquisition of new concepts. Therefore we think that our arguments for the order dependence of concepts are relevant to knowledge representation, as soon as one advances from "simple" natural language understanding to learning by being told. It is agreed that a research program that explicitly excludes learning by being told is not in need of the conceptual order dependence advocated here.

4.2 Order Dependence and Predicate Logic

In this section we will refute an argument that runs approximately as follows: formulas in predicate logic are order independent, predicate logic is the best understood way to do knowledge representation, this paper claims there should be order dependence, therefore this paper must be wrong.

The order independence that predicate logic is talking about is the independence of the result of a theorem prover from the order in which axioms and theorems are stored internally. In other words, this is a spatial order independence. We are not interested in this order independence, but in the conceptual order dependence between the objects and predicates used in these theorems and in constraints in acquiring these theorems if they involve several concepts which are previously unknown to the system.

A theorem prover does not try to understand individual concepts. This is exactly the power of logic, that one can construct programs that operate based on the form of well formed formulas, but not on their meaning. We are trying to make these formulas a better model of human intelligence by imposing additional constraints on their acquisition, which seem to agree with human behavior.

4.3 Order Dependence and Production Rules

A similar argument as for logic might be used for production rules. Production rules have been introduced originally as a cognitive model. This paper claims that a cognitive model of knowledge representation should permit to express order dependence. Production rules do not maintain an order dependence. Therefore this paper must be wrong.

Production rules, although interesting as a cognitive model, certainly do not capture all aspects of human information processing. To mention only one phenomenon that they are not addressing, it

---

[3]This term it due to Shapiro, personal communication.

is now widely agreed that short term memory and long term memory are not sufficient to model all the human cognitive abilities [21]. Conceptual order dependence of knowledge structures is simply another issue that is not addressed in rule-based (production) systems.

Frustrations with limitations of the production rule methodology have also lead to the development of deep-model based [20] expert systems. This indicates that the limitations of production systems are not limited to cognitive aspects, but extend to very practical performance issues.

4.4   Which Knowledge Needs Order Most?

Given that knowledge representation formalisms currently in use do not maintain conceptual order information the question arises whether domains differ in their need to maintain this knowledge.

Looking back at our arguments we find that we have used "definitions," "logical reasoning," and "teaching" as three indications for the need to maintain knowledge about the order of ones concepts. Defined terms should "point back" to their definitions. Results of a reasoning process should point back to the facts and rules used in their derivation, and more complicated scientific concepts should clearly refer back to the simpler concepts they are derived from. The one domain where these three types of knowledge occur most commonly together is science education.

5   Conceptual Order Dependence and Representational Primitives

Researchers in knowledge representation have covered a wide spectrum concerning the issue of "primitives." Quillian's [14] ground breaking work on semantic networks explicitly excluded the use of primitives. At the other extreme are Schank's well known [16] primitive actions. Semantic networks and representation languages of the KL-ONE family [1] are based on "epistemic primitives" [2] that control the inheritance mechanisms but are not primitives of the representation domain. In the SNePS system [17, 19] predefined primitives are limited to a small set of arcs that are the building blocks for rules, while primitives of the representation domain exist only as non conceptual relations expressed as user defined arcs.

Requiring a partial order for concepts in declarative knowledge representation raises the question whether one must have a set of primitives. We think that the answer is yes. We are not arguing for any minimal, specific, or limited set of primitives. This frees us from trying to identify such a set. Nevertheless, there are three classes of concepts that seem not to be defined in terms of other concepts. These three classes are (1) perceptual concepts, (2) emotional concepts, and (3) motoric concepts. In our representational theory these three classes of concepts function as primitives for all other concepts.

A perceptual concept is a concept which (has instances that) we can recognize without being able to explain what features permit us to recognize it. An emotional concept is a concept that describes a mental state which we cannot explain but which we can recognize. A motoric concept is a concept that describes an action that we can perform, often without being able to explain in detail how we are doing it.

The best understood of these three classes of concepts are the perceptual ones. For natural kinds, perceptual concepts have been analyzed in categorization research [15]. It is from here that we derive an argument against a limited set of primitives. People can recognize members of an unlimited number of increasingly complex categories. The fact that we cannot explain how we recognize them shows that their definition is not grounded in a declarative knowledge representation formalism, which makes it possible to think of them as primitives from the point of view of the knowledge representation system. (From the point of view of the perceptual system the recognition of complicated categories might very well be based upon procedures for recognizing instances of simple categories.)

In terms of our previously introduced metaphor, a jigsaw puzzle, the primitives correspond to the pieces at the edges of the puzzle. If we assume that the puzzle can grow unlimited to the right and up, then the left edge (the y-axis) may grow unlimited upwards, and the lower edge (the x-axis) may grow unlimited to the right. Therefore, there are primitives of the declarative knowledge representation system, but there is an unlimited number of them.[4]

5.1 Representational Primitives and Symbol Grounding

Harnad [8] has argued that AI systems that only manipulate symbols will not be able to pass the Total Turing Test, [5] and to expose real human-like intelligence. As a solution to this problem he suggests to ground symbols by a system of transducers and neural networks in observations of the real world.

What he refers to as perceptually grounded symbols corresponds to our understanding of perceptual concepts. Our assumption in this paper is that every concept must be grounded. Many concepts will be grounded perceptually, motorically, or emotionally, but many other concepts will be grounded by definitions using already grounded concepts. We refer to this process as *propositional grounding*. Concepts that are grounded by a definition containing already grounded concepts are propositionally grounded concepts.

This paper does not represent research in symbol grounding. We take it as a given fact that symbols must be grounded [6] Our question is how to represent the grounding of concepts which are not primitive (according to our definition) in a knowledge representation framework.

6 Pragmatic Reasons for other Order Dependencies

As a side note we want to point out that it has already been stated in the literature that when working with a knowledge based system there are *pragmatic* reasons **not** to insist on spatial order independence of individual knowledge structures. This is not obvious when one works with a problem that fits onto a single page, but it becomes obvious with larger problem sizes. One place where difficulties have been noticed are rule based systems like OPS-5 [4], where production rules in

---

[4]If we extend our metaphor to a 3-dimensional open ended puzzle it seems attractive to associate the directions of growth with perceptual, emotional, and motoric primitives.

[5]An extension of the Turing Test that requires interaction with the world.

[6]This fact is still the subject of heated discussions between AI researchers.

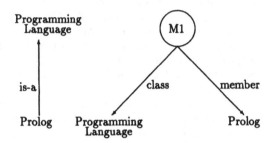

Figure 1: IS-A in KL-ONE and SNePS

principle may be given in any order. However, in practice things are more difficult, as Jackson [10] states, "Even in cases where the rules do make true categorical statements about the domain, there is no guarantee that your program will perform in the way that you expect. . . . As mentioned earlier, this is often a critical consideration when adding a new rule to the system."

When debugging an OPS-5 program, the complete independence of rules forces the programmer to potentially consider every rule in the system. The debugging task becomes considerably easier if rules that deal with closely related situations or are likely to be fired in close succession are spatially organized together.

7   An Example: IS-A Hierarchies

For an example we will use one of the best investigated phenomena in the whole field of knowledge representation, namely the is-a relation. Fig.1 shows a graphical representation for the is-a relation in two different styles. The left part shows a representation that corresponds to the members of the KL-ONE family, while the right part shows an equivalent representation for the SNePS system.

Both parts show a representation for the fact that Prolog is a programming language. The major difference is that SNePS also represents the proposition of this fact as a node, m1, while the proposition is implicit in the KL-ONE form.

Both representations, however, do not record the temporal order of acquiring the two involved concepts. It is not clear from the internal representation or the diagram, whether the concept of programming language was known before or after the concept of Prolog. Clearly one would like to maintain this information, for the reasons explained in the previous sections.

In addition, a person will often be able to remember that s/he knew the concept of programming language before learning about Prolog. If knowledge representation is trying to be cognitively valid, as we think it should, then it must be possible in principle to maintain the distinction between

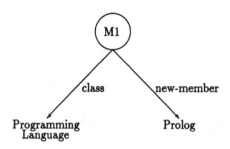

Figure 2: Distinguishing a new member.

heaving heard first about Prolog or having heard first about programming languages.

This distinction also comes out clearly from natural language utterances which could result in building the structures in Fig. 1. A sentence like "Prolog is a programming language" assumes that the hearer is already familiar with the concept of a programming language. On the other hand, a sentence like "Prolog is an example for what has been called a relational programming language" clearly introduces the class of relational programming languages and assumes that Prolog is an already known concept.

In Fig. 2 we show an alternative representation that distinguishes the new member relative to the existing class. In Fig. 3 we show another variant of Fig. 1, this time a preexisting object is associated with a new class.

This new representation raises one obvious question. Have we created unnecessary complications? Do we have to do three tests from now on to decide whether something is a member of a class, or at least two tests, to distinguish between Fig. 2 and Fig. 3? Fortunately, this is not the case, at least not if we limit ourselves to the use of the SNePS system.

The SNePS interpreter combines two systems of reasoning, a rule based reasoning facility and a path-based reasoning facility. The path-based facility permits one to describe arbitrary combinations of arcs using operators like "AND", "OR", and "KLEENE-STAR". It is similar to the original reasoning mechanism that Quillian [14] had in mind when he introduced semantic networks. Any defined path may then be used in the system for retrieval operations, as if it were just a simple arc. We will show an example run that demonstrates how this facility permits us to keep the added knowledge in the system, without complicating the retrieval operations.

```
*(define member class new-member new-class)

(MEMBER CLASS NEW-MEMBER NEW-CLASS)
```

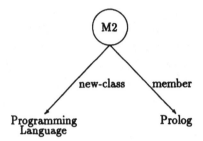

Figure 3: Distinguishing a new class.

```
*(build new-member prolog class language)

(M1)

*(build new-class programming-language member prolog)

(M2)

*(define-path member (or member new-member))

MEMBER implied by the path (OR MEMBER NEW-MEMBER)
MEMBER- implied by the path (OR MEMBER- NEW-MEMBER-)

*(define-path class (or class new-class))

CLASS implied by the path (OR CLASS NEW-CLASS)
CLASS- implied by the path (OR CLASS- NEW-CLASS-)

*(find member ?x class ?y)

(M1 M2)

*(find new-member ?z class ?a)
```

(M1)

*(find member ?b new-class ?c)

(M2)

Above test run shows an interaction with the SNePS system. Lines starting with a "*" are user input, and the "*" is the system prompt. All other lines show system replies. Timing information has been edited out for clarity. The line (define member class new-member new-class) introduces the names of all user defined arcs to the system. The line (build new-member prolog class language) creates a structure as shown in Fig.2. The command (build new-class programming-language member prolog) creates a SNePS structure as shown in Fig. 3. The line (define-path member (or member new-member)) introduces a path "member" that consists either of an arc "member" or of an arc "new-member". A similar definition is given for the path "class" in the next user input.

The last three structures show retrieval operations from the network. (find member ?x class ?y) finds any node with a member and a class arc or path emanating from it. ?x and ?y are, as usual, variables (more precisely variable nodes). The system responds with (M1 M2), in other words it has found both previously built structures, independently whether they denote a new member or a new class. On the other hand, (find new-member ?x class ?y) looks specifically for new members of an existing class.

With this example we have hopefully demonstrated what we mean by conceptual order dependence of knowledge structures, and we have also shown that a well designed system like SNePS can implement this new theory without introducing new features.

8   Part Hierarchies

Part hierarchies are another very popular representation system in AI [7]. Clearly there is no problem to carry above representational ideas over to them. Instead of building a network structure with two arcs "member class" we can build a network structure with two arcs "part whole". We can then introduce alternative arcs "new-part" and "new-whole" and use them to maintain order dependence in the network. Finally, using two disjunctive path definitions that combine part and new-part into one path, and whole and new-whole into another path, we can retrieve any part assertion, independently of the conceptual order in which part and whole are maintained. Still, the knowledge of the order is in the system and may be accessed.

The other question is whether people actually remember in which order they acquire part relations. According to our intuition this is often the case. For technical devices we can usually tell that we first knew the device and later on learned about its parts. For clusters of objects we often know the parts before we acquire the term for the whole. In this sense we know about books before we learn about libraries, and about cows before we learn about cattle herds.

9 Open Problems

A large number of open problems is left to deal with. For instance, it is not clear whether our formalism represents a real gain in representational power, or whether it could be simulated with other known representational tools. Similarly it is not clear for which relations order dependence is represented, and how the cognitive system decides when to maintain it, and when to ignore it.

Also, a number of possible counter arguments have not been dealt with yet. For instance, a teacher can reorganize the material in his lecture. Our representation so far does not account for this phenomenon. This problem and related questions, such as similarities between our formalism and "temporal logics," will have to be dealt with in future work.

10 Conclusions

In this paper we have distinguished between three different senses of the term "order independence of declarative knowledge." We have argued that people are able to remember to some degree the order in which they acquire concepts. We refer to this order as conceptual order. A cognitively valid knowledge representation formalism that can deal with knowledge acquisition needs the ability to maintain this order.

We have collected arguments to support the need for ordered knowledge. For instance, the ability of a teacher to organize his knowledge in an order such that certain items are dependent on specific other items is an indication that some order is maintained in the human knowledge representation system. We have also argued, that natural language processing, if it advances to the level of learning by being told, needs to maintain conceptual order information.

Connections between our theory and the symbol grounding problem were discussed. The best way to view this work from the symbol grounding paradigm is to consider it as an approach to propositional grounding which relies that primitive concepts are grounded perceptually.

Two widely investigated relations, the part-of and the is-a relation, have been used as examples how to formulate class membership and part relation in a way such that the conceptual order is maintained in the semantic knowledge of the system. Finally we have shown that the SNePS semantic network processing system can support the distinctions imposed by conceptual order, without complicating the retrieval of the basic facts and without changing the SNePS theory or interpreter.

Acknowledgements

Many thanks to Deepak Kumar, for organizing the first SNePS workshop, Stuart Shapiro, Terry Nutter, Bill Rapaport, and Ernesto Morgado for commenting on the presentation of an earlier version of this paper, Stevan Harnad for personal help with the symbol grounding theory, and Yehoshua Perl, for paying my trip to the workshop from his grant.

References

[1] R. J. Brachman and J. Schmolze. An overview of the KL-ONE knowledge representation system. *Cognitive Science*, 9(2):171–216, 1985.

[2] Ronald J. Brachman. On the epistemological status of semantic networks. In Nicholas Findler, editor, *Associative Networks*. Academic Press, New York, 1979.

[3] Ronald J. Brachman and Hector J. Levesque. *Readings in Knowledge Representation*. Morgan Kaufmann Publishers Inc., Los Altos, California, 1985.

[4] L. Brownston, R. Farrell, E. Kant, and N. Martin. *Programming Expert Systems in OPS5*. Addison-Wesley, Reading, MA, 1985.

[5] Herbert H. Clark and Eve V. Clark. *Psychology and Language*. Harcourt Brace Jovanovic, New York, 1977.

[6] J. Doyle. A glimpse of truth-maintenance. In P. H. Winston and R. H. Brown, editors, *Artificial Intelligence: An MIT Perspective*, pages 119–135. The MIT Press, Cambridge, MA, 1982.

[7] James Geller. *A Knowledge Representation Theory for Natural Language Graphics*. PhD thesis, SUNY at Buffalo, CS Department, 1988.

[8] Stevan Harnad. The symbol grounding problem. *Physica D*, forthcoming.

[9] Eduard H. Hovy. Planning coherent multisentential text. In *26th Annual Meeting of the Association for Computational Lingusitics*, pages 163–169. ACL, 1988.

[10] Peter Jackson. *Introduction to Expert Systems*. Addison-Wesley, Reading, MA, 1986.

[11] Douglas B. Lenat and Edward A. Feigenbaum. On the thresholds of knowledge. In *Proceedings of the tenth International Joint Conference on Artificial Intelligence*, pages 1173–1182, Los Altos, CA, 1987. Morgan Kaufman Publishers.

[12] John McCarthy. Programs with common sense. In M. Minsky, editor, *Semantic Information Processing*, pages 403–418. The MIT Press, Cambridge, MA, 1968.

[13] J. Pitrat. Declarative knowledge representation. In L. Bolc, editor, *Natural Language Processing*, pages 93–135. Springer Verlag, New York, 1987.

[14] M. Ross Quillian. Semantic memory. In Marvin L. Minsky, editor, *Semantic Information Processing*, pages 227–270. The MIT Press, 1968.

[15] Eleanor Rosch. Principles of categorization. In Eleanor Rosch and Barbara Lloyd, editors, *Cognition and Categorization*, pages 27–48. Lawrence Erlbaum, 1978.

[16] R. C. Schank. *Conceptual Information Processing*. North-Holland Publishing Company, 1975.

[17] Stuart C. Shapiro. The sneps semantic network processing system. In Nicholas V. Findler, editor, *Associative Networks: The Representation and use of Knowledge by Computers*, pages 179–203. Academic Press, New York, 1979.

[18] Stuart C. Shapiro and Anthony S. Maida. Intensional concepts in propositional semantic networks. *Cognitive Science*, 6:170–189, 1982.

[19] Stuart C. Shapiro and William J. Rapaport. Sneps considered as a fully intensional propositional semantic network. In Nick Cercone and Gordon McCalla, editors, *The Knowledge Frontier*, pages 262–315. Springer Verlag, New York, 1987.

[20] Stuart C. Shapiro, Sargur N. Srihari, Ming-Ruey Taie, and James Geller. Vmes: A network based versatile maintenance expert system. In *Proc. of 1st International Conference on Applications of AI to Engineering Problems*, pages 925–936, New York, April 1986. Springer Verlag.

[21] E. Tulving. *Elements of Episodic Memory*. Clarendon, Oxford, UK, 1983.

[22] R. M. Weischedel. Knowledge representation and natural language processing. *Proceedings of the IEEE*, 74(7):905–920, 1986.

[23] Joseph Weizenbaum. Eliza-a computer program for the study of natural language communication between man and machine. *Communications of the ACM*, 9(1):36–45, 1966.

An Integrated Model of Acting and Inference

Deepak Kumar
Department of Computer Science
State University of New York at Buffalo
226 Bell Hall
Buffalo, NY 14260
(716) 636-2193
kumard@cs.buffalo.edu

Abstract

This paper discusses propositional representations for representing beliefs, actions, and plans. From the point of integrating inference and acting, it introduces the notions of a *transformer*. A transformer is a representation that specifies a belief/act transformation under the influence of a transforming procedure. We will look at forward and backward transforming procedures. Under this scheme a reasoning rule in SNePS is a belief-belief transformer, i.e. it is a specification of antecedent and consequent beliefs. Such a transformer can be used in forward as well as backward inference (using the transformation procedures). Similarly, we can have belief-action, action-belief, and action-action transformers. These transformers can be used to model planning, plan decompositions, sequencing of actions, effects and preconditions of actions, and reactivity to sensory input. While some of these transformers can be uniformly used by both forward as well as backward transformation procedures, it is not desirable to do so. For this reason we need different representations for same transformers so that some transformations can be blocked. We informally outline a scheme for modifying the existing inference procedure (SNIP) to do forward/backward transformations involved in reasoning as well as acting.

1 Introduction

This paper reviews current models of acting and inference from the perspective of building AI models of rational cognitive agents. Among other things rational cognitive agents can plan, act, and reason about a world based on their beliefs. Rational agents should be endowed with senses and act in multi-agent worlds. An agent in a multi-agent world needs to be able to infer the beliefs, goals, and intentions of other agents (see [Appelt, 1985; Cohen and Levesque, 1985; Pollack, 1986]). A more important prerequisite is the ability of the agent to keep an updated world model (set of beliefs) that accounts for its own actions as well as those of others at all times. Reacting to changes in the world is an other important consideration for a rational agent. While there are systems that exhibit these capabilities, we claim that they are not good models of rational agents. This paper discusses why this is so and proposes an integrated paradigm within which one can build models of rational cognitive agents.

2   Current Approaches

A modeled agent should be capable of acting, reasoning as well as discussing *all* aspects of acting and reasoning. Research in planning and acting has progressed independently of the research in knowledge representation and reasoning. While it is good to maintain this dichotomy to focus on specific issues, it turns out that knowledge representation and reasoning capabilities of current planners/actors are restricted to providing basic access to a world model that can be used by a procedural planning component. Traditional planners end up using three different levels of representations (each using a different representation language)—a representation for world model (typically a FOPL); a representation for operators/actions (like the operator schema of STRIPS [Fikes and Nilsson, 1971], or the operator description language—ODL of SIPE [Wilkins, 1988]); and a representation for plans (like NOAH's [Sacerdoti, 1977] and SIPE's procedural networks). As a consequence, the system has to perform reasoning at three different levels—reasoning within the world model (done by the so called *truth criterion procedure* in SIPE); reasoning about actions (used in the planning component); and reasoning about plans (as done by *procedural critics* of NOAH and SIPE).

Facts stored in the world model correspond to the agent's beliefs. The kind of reasoning done on these beliefs is limited to basic retrieval, and sometimes, using simple inference rules (which may or may not be expressed in the same language! See [Wilkins, 1988]'s deductive operators.) simple consequences of current beliefs can be derived. The state of the art in knowledge representation and reasoning is much more advanced than that. Current knowledge representation and reasoning systems are capable of dealing with issues in natural language understanding, representing beliefs of the agent as well as others, belief revision using truth maintenance procedures, and other subtle issues. Some of these representations also deal with beliefs about agents performing actions and events taking place.

A survey of various planning/acting systems and various knowledge representation systems reveals that in most systems it is awkward to do acting in logic-based systems (but it is convenient to talk about representation and research issues), and it is awkward to research representation and reasoning issues in systems designed for planning/acting. This is also expressed in the following quote from [Georgeff, 1987]:

> Another promising approach to providing the kind of high-level goal-directed reasoning capabilities, together with the reactivity required for survival in the real world, is to consider planning systems as rational agents that are endowed with the psychological attitudes of belief, desire, and intention. The problem that then arises is specifying the properties we expect of these attitudes, the way they interrelate, and the ways they determine rational behavior in a situated agent.

We have designed and implemented representations for plans and acts for SNePS—an intensional propositional knowledge representation and reasoning system[Shapiro, 1979; Shapiro and Rapaport, 1987; Shapiro and Group, 1989]. This system, called SNACTor (for the SNePS ACTor) is described in [Kumar *et al.*, 1988; Shapiro *et al.*, 1989a; Shapiro *et al.*, 1989b]. We will discuss the characteristics of this system in light of the comments made above after a brief overview.

2.1 The SNePS Actor

The architecture of the SNePS actor is as shown in Figure 2.1. The SNePS actor operates in a

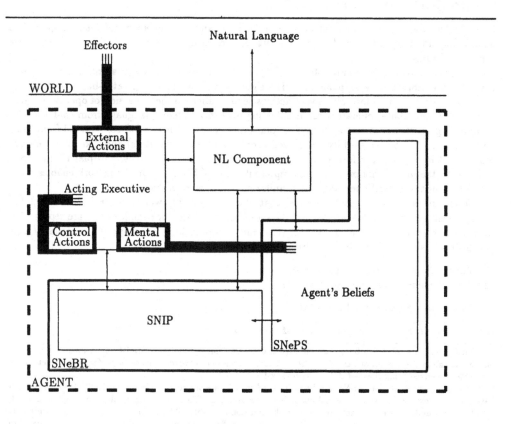

Figure 1: Architecture of The SNePS Actor

world inhabited by itself (i.e. a single-agent world). The agent has beliefs that are stored as SNePS propositions in the agent's belief space (called a SNeBR context, see [Martins and Shapiro, 1988]). SNeBR—the SNePS system for Belief Revision, an assumption-based truth maintenance system [Martins and Shapiro, 1986b; Martins and Shapiro, 1986a; Martins and Shapiro, 1988] ensures that the agent's belief space is always consistent[1]. All interaction with the agent is done using the natural language component. Sentences are parsed by a grammar (written in ATN) and translated into SNePSUL(—the SNePS User Language) commands and form beliefs in the agent's belief space. World model rules for reasoning in the agent's belief space are also translated and represented as agent's beliefs. An inference rule in SNePS is a structured proposition node of the form[2]

```
AntCq(<ant-beliefs>, <cq-beliefs>)
```

Roughly, the above rule is a specification of antecedent and consequent beliefs using appropriate quantifiers and connectives. SNIP can do forward, backward, or bidirectional inference using the same set of rules.

We treat acts/plans as mental objects. This enables the agent to discuss, formulate, use, recognize, and reason about acts/plans. This is a significant advance over operator-based descriptions of plans. Operator-based formulations of actions tend to alienate the discussion of operators themselves. As noted above, operators are usually specified in a different language from that used for representing beliefs about states. Moreover, plans (or procedural networks) constructed from these operators can only be accessed by specialized programs (critics, executors) and, like operators, are represented in still another formalism. Our representations for acts, goals, and plans build upon and add to the intensional propositional representations of SNePS. This framework enables us to tackle various tasks mentioned above in a uniform and coherent fashion.

We classify actions as being *external*—that affect the outside world; *control*—that affect the acting executive; and *mental*—that affect the set of beliefs. Plans (or complex acts) are represented as structured nodes comprising a set of external and control actions. Decompositions of plans/goals are specified using the following predicates[3]

```
PlanGoal( <some-plan>, <some-goal>)
PlanAct( <some-plan>, <complex-act>)
```

Effects of acts are represented using the

```
ActEffect( <some-act-i>, <effects-of-act-i>)
```

---

[1]During the course of acting beliefs are removed and added. This is done using SNeBR operations. For example, one of the things SNeBR takes care of is when a belief is removed as a consequence of performing an action, all propositions derived using that belief are also removed.

[2]This linear representation of SNePS rules is designed to facilitate our current discussion. In SNePS rules one can have universal, existential, and numerical quantifiers over variables. The connectives available are and-entailment, or-entailment, numerical entailment, and-or, thresh, and non-derivable. The predicate used here represents only the typical antecedent-consequent type of rules. However, the discussion applies to all SNePS rules in general. See [Shapiro and Group, 1989] for details on the SNePS representation of rules.

[3]As in the case of rules, this representation is being used to facilitate discussion at a general level. Each predicate mentioned here is represented as a structured proposition node. The exact syntax and semantics of these representations can be found in [Kumar *et al.*, 1988; Shapiro *et al.*, 1989b]

predicate. This predicate specifies mental actions of believing to be performed so as to update the set of beliefs after performing an act. Acts can also have preconditions that are specified using the

```
PreconditionAct( <preconditions-of-act-i>, <some-act-i>)
```

predicate.

Requests to perform an action are serviced by the acting executive (see Figure 2.1). The request (which is represented as an act node) gets scheduled on an acting queue maintained by the executive. This represents the agent's intentions. Plans are structured using *control actions* that when interpreted affect the queue of intentions. Our repertoire of control actions includes sequencing (**snsequence**), conditional (**snif**), iteration (**sniterate**), and a few others (see [Kumar *et al.*, 1988]). *External actions* affect the external world via their respective associated procedures. The acting executive uses SNIP to derive plans, plan decompositions, and the effects and preconditions of actions. It schedules *mental actions* to believe effects of actions. It also schedules acts to achieve preconditions of actions in case they are not satisfied.

2.2   The SNePS Inference Package

SNIP, the SNePS Inference Package[Hull, 1986; Ferreira *et al.*, 1989], is implemented on top of MULTI(—A LISP based Multiprocessing system) [McKay and Shapiro, 1980]. MULTI is a simulated multiprocessing system. It maintains a queue of parallel processes. It executes processes from the process queue until the queue is empty. An inference is carried out by SNIP by activating a node[4] as an appropriate process. Executing such processes may result in requests or reports to other node processes in the system. When a requesting process receives a report it had asked for, a conclusion is drawn and added as a derived belief to the belief space. This completes an inference. As mentioned earlier, SNIP can perform forward, backward, and bidirectional inference.

2.3   Comments on the SNePS Actor

There are some similarities that can be made between the architecture of the SNePS actor and the inference package. As first suggested by [Morgado and Shapiro, 1983] inference can be looked at as the sequence of actions performed in applying rules to derive beliefs from other beliefs. In the SNePS actor model, this can be represented as a mental action. Thus SNIP can be viewed as a *mental actor*.

Before we examine consequences of the above observation, let us first observe some other aspects of the SNePS acting system. First, as has already been pointed out, the SNePS actor is a model of an agent which is a "pure affector" that lives in a world populated only by itself. However, a rational agent has to be able to act in a real world inhabited by other agents (affector systems). Also, the world is being affected by the constant occurrence of natural phenomena. To account for these, rational agents should be endowed with sensory capabilities so they can update their beliefs about the world. Regardless of the sensory interface between the agent and the world, sensory information

---

[4]In the case of forward inference the node is the belief to be added to the belief space of the agent. In the case of backward inference it is the node representing the query

results in the formation of new beliefs. These beliefs are acquired on a continuous basis. Of course there can also be sensory activity intended by the agent in order to gain some information. A model of a rational agent should be able to account for both these types of sensory activity.

A model of attention is required to filter through beliefs acquired by sensory activity. As a consequence, some beliefs will simply be added to the agent's belief space. However, adding of some beliefs may require the agent to perform some reactive actions. An agent's reactions are governed by its "desires". Thus there is a need for a model that can use the beliefs and desires of an agent to create new intentions to perform some actions.

Ensuing from above remarks and the observation that inference can be viewed as a specialized forms of acting is the suggestion that acting and inference are closely related. In what follows, we build an integrated model of acting and inference based on these ideas.

3   Integrating Acting and Inference

Earlier, we introduced the notion of mental actions that are used to update/retrieve an agent's beliefs. This enables us to establish a closer relationship between rules of inference and rules of acting (or planning). Believing is a state of knowledge; acting is the process of changing one state into another. Reasoning rules pass a *truth* or a *belief* status from antecedent to consequent, whereas acting rules pass an *intention* status from earlier acts to later acts. A reasoning rule can be viewed as as rule specifying an act—that of believing some previously non-believed proposition, but the believe action is already included in the semantics of the propositional connective. As mentioned in [Shapiro, 1989] when a rule fires the agent forms the intention of believing its consequences. This suggests that we can integrate our models of inference and acting by eliminating the acting executive. The inference queue *is* the queue of intentions. While this clarifies the notion of an inference rule as specifying an act, we need to reexamine our representation for plans and acts and the role they play under the influence of forward/backward chaining procedures. For that purpose, we first introduce a more general notion of a transformer.

4   Transformers

A *transformer* is a representation that specifies a belief/act transformation under the influence of a transformation procedure. It has two parts—$(< a >, < b >)$, where both $< a >$ and $< b >$ can specify either a set of beliefs or some act. Basically a transformer is a more general notation that captures the notions of reasoning as well as acting. The transformation procedure can use the transformer in forward as well as backward chaining fashion. Using a transformer in forward chaining is equivalent to the interpretation "after the agent believes/performs $< a >$, it believes/performs $< b >$." A transformation procedure using backward chaining on a transformer yields the interpretation "if the agent wants to believe/perform $< b >$, it must believe/perform $< a >$."

Since both $< a >$ and $< b >$ can be sets of beliefs or an act, we have four types of transformers—*belief-belief; belief-action; action-belief;* and *action-action*. The idea of defining a transformer is to have a unified notion of reasoning and acting. We will try to classify our representations as transformers and the role they play in planning, acting, and reasoning.

4.1 Transformers for Reasoning

Belief-belief transformers are reasoning rules of SNePS. As noted before, a reasoning rule (AntCq) can be used in forward, backward, or bidirectional inference. The meaning and use of the representation remains the same. SNIP already knows how to interpret these.

4.2 Belief-act Transformers

Consider the transformer

```
WhenDo( <some-belief>, <some-act>)
```

Under forward chaining, this transformer can be interpreted as "after the agent believes <some--belief>, it performs <some-act>[5]". Such a transformer models reactivity. E.g., a reactivity specification like "In the case of a fire leave building" can be represented as a WhenDo transformer. When a sensory input yields a belief that there is a fire, a forward chaining procedure will use the transformer to schedule the act of leaving the building on the queue of intentions.

Used during backward chaining, i.e. "if the agent wants to perform <some-act>, it must believe <some-belief>," the WhenDo transformer seems to represent a specification of a precondition of an action. This is clearly undesirable. In the reactivity example, for instance, every time it has to leave the building, the agent would try to achieve that there is a fire! Still there is a need for specifying preconditions of actions. We will use the PreconditionAct predicate as a transformer to achieve that. The transformation procedures should ensure that backward chaining is blocked in the case of WhenDo and forward chaining is blocked in the case of PreconditionAct.

4.3 Action-belief Transformers

The ActEffect and the PlanGoal propositions are *action-belief* transformers. Forward chaining through the ActEffect transformer specifies the updating of beliefs after performing an action, and backward chaining through it can be used in planning (i.e. "if the agent wants to believe <some-belief>, it must perform <some-act>."

The PlanGoal transformer used by the backward chaining procedure specifies plan decompositions for achieving some goals. Forward chaining through it is blocked.

4.4 Action-action Transformers

An *action-action* transformer is modeled using the control action snsequence. Such a transformer is used only in the forward chaining direction. It wouldn't make sense to backward chain though

---

[5]Actually, the agent will form the intention of performing <some-act>, depending on the status of intentions it may or may not be performed.

such a transformer. However, the `PlanAct` transformer, when used in backward chaining will result in specification of decomposition of complex acts.

5 The SNePS Acting and Inference Package

We have informally described the notion of a transformer as a general representation that can provide reasoning, planning, and acting capabilities under the interpretation of forward and backward chaining procedures. The resulting architecture of such a model is depicted in Figure 2. The natural

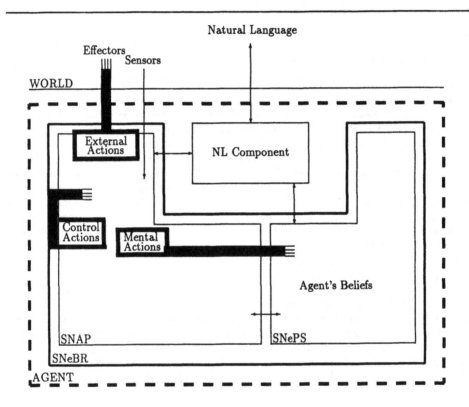

Figure 2: Architecture of the integrated acting and reasoning system.

language component and representation of agent's beliefs remains the same as that of the SNePS actor. The syntax of rules, and other planning/acting related propositions remains the same. However, they now belong to the more general class transformers. There is no need to have a separate acting executive and an inference engine. Transformers are interpreted and used by the SNePS acting and inference package which is a modified version of SNIP. The inference queue of SNIP is now the acting and inference queue[6]. In addition to existing SNIP processes (that facilitate inference), we will also have act processes that when scheduled on the queue represent the agent's intentions to perform those actions. The table below shows all the transformers and when they are activated (i.e. during forward and backward chaining).

Transformers	Forward Chaining	Backward Chaining
belief-belief	AntCq	AntCq
belief-action	WhenDo	PreconditionAct
action-belief	ActEffect	PlanGoal,ActEffect
action-action	snsequence	PlanAct

6 Conclusion

We started the paper by pointing out that most current systems use three levels of representations and reasoning. As a consequence the modeled agent, though capable of carrying out required tasks, is not able to discuss all levels of representations. We solved that problem in the model of the SNePS actor by designing and implementing intensional propositional representations of plans and acts. We treat plans and acts as mental objects so the agent can have beliefs about them just like it can have beliefs about other objects. Propositional representations also help us get rid of the notion of *planning operators*. There is no need for it. Control actions enable us to represent a complete plan as an intensional concept that can be discussed by the agent just like any other concept. The acting executive interprets these representations and maintains a queue of intentions. The system uses an ATMS to maintain a consistent belief space at all times. We expressed the desire to model an agent that would account for and react to sensory input and actions of other agents. Rather than building a reactivity module, we reexamined the architecture of the SNePS actor, and realized that the notion of a mental action used by the actor can be extended to the inference engine. We identified that reasoning rules specify an implicit act of believing and went on to suggest an integrated model of acting and inference. We informally described the notion of a transformer and how various representations fall under various types of transformers. We described the role played by these representations in reasoning and acting under the influence of forward and backward chaining procedures. The resulting model is much cleaner and reflects a close relationship between inference and acting. The issues of dealing with sensory input and reactivity are easily dealt with in this model. The resulting system is an integrated state-of-the-art acting and representation and reasoning system.

---

[6]Since we have identified that reasoning is a kind of action, and firing of reasoning rules implicitly includes the believe mental action, it is basically an acting queue. However, to stress the fact that the package is doing both acting and inference, in the classical sense, we will continue to call it the acting and inference queue, and the package an acting and inference package.

References

[Appelt, 1985] Douglas E. Appelt. Planning english refering expressions. *Artificial Intelligence*, 26:1–34, 1985.

[Cohen and Levesque, 1985] Paul R. Cohen and Hector J. Levesque. Speech acts and the recognition of shared plans. In *Proeedings of the twenty-third conference of ACL*, pages 44–59, 1985.

[Ferreira *et al.*, 1989] Carlos P. Ferreira, Nuno J. Mamede, and Joao P. Martins. *SNIP 2.1 — The SNePS Inference Package*. Technical Report, Instituto Superior Technico, 1989. In preparation.

[Fikes and Nilsson, 1971] Richard E. Fikes and Nils J. Nilsson. STRIPS: A new approach to the application of theorem proving to problem solving. *Artificial Intelligence*, 5:189–208, 1971.

[Georgeff, 1987] Michael P. Georgeff. Planning. In *Annual Reviews of Computer Science Volume 2*, pages 359–400, Annual Reviews Inc., Palo Alto, CA, 1987.

[Hull, 1986] R. G. Hull. *A New Design for SNIP the SNePS Inference Packag*. SNeRG Technical Note 14, Department of Computer Science, SUNY at Buffalo, 1986.

[Kumar *et al.*, 1988] D. Kumar, S. Ali, and S. C. Shapiro. Discussing, using and recognizing plans in SNePS preliminary report - SNACTor: an acting system. In *Proceedings of the Seventh Biennial Convention of South East Asia Regional Confederation*, pages 177–182, Tata McGraw-Hill, New Delhi, India, 1988.

[Martins and Shapiro, 1986a] J. P. Martins and S. C. Shapiro. Belief revision in SNePS. In *Proceedings of the Sixth Canadian Conference on Artificial Intelligence*, pages 230–234, Presses de l'Université du Québec, 1986.

[Martins and Shapiro, 1986b] J. P. Martins and S. C. Shapiro. Theoretical foundations for belief revision. In J. Y. Halpern, editor, *Theoretical Aspects of Reasoning About Knowledge*, pages 383–398, Morgan Kaufmann Publishers, Los Altos, CA, 1986.

[Martins and Shapiro, 1988] J. P. Martins and S. C. Shapiro. A model for belief revision. *Artificial Intelligence*, 35(1):25–79, 1988.

[McKay and Shapiro, 1980] * D. P. McKay and S. C. Shapiro. *MULTI: A LISP Based Multiprocessing System*. Technical Report 164, Department of Computer Science, SUNY at Buffalo, 1980. (Contains appendices not in LISP conference version).

[Morgado and Shapiro, 1983] E. J. Morgado and S. C. Shapiro. *Believing and Acting: An Approach to Meta-Knowledge and Meta-Reasoning*. SNeRG Technical Note 11, Department of Computer Science, SUNY at Buffalo, 1983.

[Pollack, 1986] Martha E. Pollack. *Inferring domain plans in question answering*. PhD thesis, University of Pennsylvania, 1986.

[Sacerdoti, 1977] Earl D. Sacerdoti. *A Structure for Plans and Behavior*. Elsevier North Holland, New York, NY, 1977.

[Shapiro, 1979] S. C. Shapiro. The SNePS semantic network processing system. In N. V. Findler, editor, *Associative Networks: The Representation and Use of Knowledge by Computers*, pages 179–203, Academic Press, New York, 1979.

[Shapiro, 1989] S. C. Shapiro. Formal foundations of an intensional propositional semantic network. 1989. Presented at the Workshop on Formal Aspects of Semantic Networks, Santa Catalina Island, CA.

[Shapiro and Group, 1989] S. C. Shapiro and The SNePS Implementation Group. *SNePS-2 User's Manual*. Department of Computer Science, SUNY at Buffalo, 1989.

[Shapiro and Rapaport, 1987] S. C. Shapiro and W. J. Rapaport. SNePS considered as a fully intensional propositional semantic network. In N. Cercone and G. McCalla, editors, *The Knowledge Frontier*, pages 263–315, Springer-Verlag, New York, 1987.

[Shapiro et al., 1989a] Stuart C. Shapiro, Deepak Kumar, and Syed S. Ali. A propositional network approach to plans and plan recognition. In *Proceedings of the AAAI-88 Workshop on Plan Recognition*, Morgan Kaufmann, 1989. To appear.

[Shapiro et al., 1989b] Stuart C. Shapiro, Beverly Woolf, Deepak Kumar, Syed S. Ali, Penelope Sibun, David Forster, and Scott Anderson. *Discussing, Using, and Recognizing Plans–Annual Report for 1988*. Technical Report, North-East Artificial Intelligence Consortium, 1989.

[Wilkins, 1988] David E. Wilkins. *Practical Planning–Extending the Classical AI Planning Paradigm*. Morgan Kaufmann, Palo Alto, CA, 1988.

The Structure of Agency:
Issues in the Representation of Agency and Action

Randall R. Dipert

Department of Philosophy

SUNY Fredonia, Fredonia NY 14063

E-mail: dipert@cs.buffalo.edu, dipert@snyfreba.bitnet

In this essay, I will attempt to characterize the notions of agent, agency, and action.[1] Although I will draw heavily upon recent and classical work in philosophical action theory, my main goal is to present a theory with enough detail that part or possibly even all of its features could be represented in an artificial system. As good a place to begin as any is with a recent book by Michael Bratman, *Intention, Plans, and Practical Reason* [Bratman 1987] that has deservedly attracted considerable attention. Bratman presented there a "functional" analysis of the role intentions and plans play in human action. (See also [Bratman and Lansky 1986], and [Brand *et al.* 1989]). Very broadly described, Bratman argues that intentions play three roles: (1) they **initiate** practical reasoning, such as planning, about how to accomplish the goal, (2) they **inhibit** further deliberation about whether to achieve the intended goal, and (3) when signaled and the intentions of others are recognized, they **coordinate** effort.[2]

---

[1]The research herein described was begun under the auspices of a Research Opportunity Award (ROA, 1986) from the National Science Foundation as part of grant IST-8504713, W.J. Rapaport, "Logical Foundations for Belief Representation," and continued under an award (1988-89) in Graduate and Research Initiative (GRI) Visiting Professor Program at SUNY at Buffalo. I have profited from conversations from, correspondence with, and comments by W.J. Rapaport, H.N. Castañeda, S.C. Shapiro, and M. Bratman.

[2]Agency, intention, responsibility, and action are in fact usually considered to be intimately related notions. Agents are entities capable of having intentions. Actions are the behavior of agents that were brought about by intentions. Saying an entity is responsible for behavior—and then subject to praise or blame—entails that the entity is an agent, and intended or was capable of intentionally bringing about the behavior. For a formulation of Bratman's theory and additions to it, see [Cohen and Levesque 1987]. Cohen and Levesque add these five characteristics to Bratman's 3: (4) The agent believes p (the intended action) is possible, (5) The agent does not believe that he will not bring about p, (6) Under certain conditions, the agent believes that he will bring about p, (7) Agents need not intend all the expected side-effects of their intentions, and (my paraphrase) (8) Agents are disposed to persist in attempts to achieve p. However, *desiderata* (4), (5), and (6) seem to be more a feature of *rational* behavior, or a feature of ideal agency, than of agency *simpliciter*. The need to guard against item (7) would seem to be an artifact of working in the "wrong"—e.g., non-intensional—knowledge representation schemes. Item (8) falls prey to some of the same objections I bring to bear against Bratman, namely, that 1-8 are not sufficient for intention, and that (8)

If there is a weakness in Bratman's account, it is in the very central issue with which he works: agency. For example, in what sense could his characterization be said to have given the necessary and sufficient conditions for agency, for "rational action" as opposed to rationally-coordinated and rational-appearing behavior?[3] On the one hand, it seems rather clear that we can at this very moment construct artificial systems with the three characteristics of intentions Bratman formulates: in a knowledge-representation scheme we could have mechanisms that initiate planning, chill further deliberation, and both signal and search to recognize other "agents' " intentions. But given their gross simplicity, no one, I think, would be tempted to say we would then automatically have a full-fledged case of agency, or that any resulting behavior constitutes "action" for which the "agent" is responsible. So Bratman's three characteristics do not seem to be *sufficient* for agency. (It is then a good question whether they are sufficient for characterizing intentions, since how could we have intentions without an agent, an intend*er*, in the proper relationship to these data-objects or states?)

Furthermore, we can well imagine an entity lacking some of the rationality in planning Bratman so carefully describes, or of occasionally, even willfully, not planning precisely how to go about what the agent has intended, or in cheerfully reconsidering and redeliberating some or many of the already decided-upon "intentions." But such a sporting, if inefficient, entity could still be an agent, it would seem. Consequently, many of the features Bratman (as well as Levesque) attributes to intention, do not seem *necessary*, for agency either. Complete rationality, decisiveness, "follow through," and transparency of intentions had better *not* be requirements for agency, or we are sure to lose all of our paradigmatic agents, save God![4] In the remainder of this essay, I will develop a theory of what I argue are some of the necessary features of intention, action, and agency. I will also remark upon what I think are characteristics of "typically human" agency.[5] In doing so, I will be attempting to fill a long-standing gap. Namely, remarkably few philosophers have attempted to characterize, or to define necessary and sufficient conditions for, the basic notions of action, intention, and so on—although assumptions about the nature of action have long played an important role in philosophy, especially in ethics. The account will rely on contributions by Aristotle,

---

in particular is not a necessary condition of an intention: we can conceive of flawed agents who do not persist in one or more intention (although we perhaps cannot imagine an agent who persists in none of his "intentions.")

[3]One of the methodological flaws of many applications of "functionalism" in cognitive science seems to be the temptation to content oneself with "some observations" about the role a notion plays, without regard either to the salience/basicness of the observations, or to their completeness. Bratman does not seem especially concerned with either aspect in his analysis: he does not seem to be especially concerned with the "level of explanation" his characterization addresses, nor (even more clearly) with its completeness in characterizing intention, agency, etc. In his defense, he does not claim for his theory either the status of a foundational analysis nor that of adequacy/completeness. Furthermore, one would have to admit that this modesty is appropriate to the discipline—rigorous analysis of agency, intention, and action—which is in its infancy.

[4]And while God is a limiting case on some of these counts, he is certainly not so in the extent to which he makes his intentions clear. For an account of special communicative intentions, whose fulfillment consists in their recognition by others, see [Dipert 1986].

[5]I assume that what is necessarily true of agency is true of human agency. But what may be necessary or widespread for human agency may not be necessary for agency *simpliciter*. Bratman, incidentally, suggests that some of the features of human agency, including certain features of human planning, are implications of human cognitive finitude.

Castañeda, Brand, Bratman, and others, although I will not fuss over its precise genealogy. As a methodological principle, I too will here adopt a "functional" approach. However, I believe a good, broad functional account of a cognitive activity or object would include not just its relationships with objects and processes "internal" to the agent, but also broader historical and sociological relationships. (I develop this theory in [Dipert 1989]. See also [Putnam 1988].)

I will also be making certain bold assumptions about the representability of objects of cognitive attitudes[6] that fall broadly within the intensional, "objects of thought" school, as well as about the nature of the operations performed on these objects. (See [Rapaport, 1986], [Shapiro and Rapaport, 1987].) If other accounts, such as materialistic/neurological, neural network, connectionist, or other paradigms, are adequate or correct, I assume that what I say can be translated into this theory, and am not here eager to debate the metaphysical foundations since, I think, so little of what I say hangs on it—other than my style of presentation. The precise paradigm that I assume, but will not fully utilize, is the theory of representing intensional entities that one sees in the SNePS (Semantic Network Processing System) account. (See [Shapiro 1979], [Shapiro and Rapaport 1987] and [Maida and Shapiro 1982].) This is probably not trivial, since I think one of the weaknesses of Bratman's account arises because of his attempt to be neutral among semantic representation schemes; this leads to a lack of detail in his examples of what precisely is intended, believed, and so on—when some of the puzzles he presents may be resolvable by a fine-grained analysis of representational questions rather than by invoking elaborate constraints on rationality.[7]

I

I will assume that wishes and desires are primarily directed to propositions, states of affairs, or portions thereof, and that these typically do not themselves utilize concepts of agents or agency. That is, they are representations of desired states or conditions of the (non-agent) world. On the other hand, I will assume that intentions and other action-theoretic attitudes are primarily directed to cognitive objects that *do* invoke notions of agents or agency. That is we have attitudes toward cognitive objects that crucially include a representation of a role for agents. Intention, persuasion, cooperation and communication are such notions, since they require attitudes toward conceptual objects (myself or others) whose status as an agent is significant. An action-theoretic attitude, such as an intention, can be directed toward a cognitive object whose subject is myself, an unspecified

---

[6]By the phrase 'cognitive attitudes' I mean to include propositional attitudes, attitudes directed toward the concepts of objects, e.g., fear and other emotions, as well as attitudes toward activities, actions, and so on, that *might* be distinct from propositions.

[7]Thus one can look closely at the case of a log blocking a driveway [Bratman 1987: 39], and see a number of points of lack of specificity on crucial representational questions: "Suppose there is a log blocking my driveway; and suppose I intend to move the log this morning but believe that since it is too heavy I will not move it.... So I add an intention to have the tree company move the log this afternoon. So my plan for the day includes my moving the log this morning and my having the tree company move it this afternoon. But it seems folly to plan to cause the log to be moved twice." Did I at first intend *myself* physically to move the log? Or did I intend that the log "be gone" (an intended *state*) or that it "be moved" (an intended activity with an unspecified agent), or perhaps that I bring it about that some agent—possibly myself—move it? Was the vague intention "to move the log" *refined* (instantiating the "someone" to the tree company) or was it *revised* (replacing "myself" with "the tree company")? Although this may sound a bit harsh, a large number of Bratman's concrete examples of beliefs and intentions involve a lack of specificity over what precisely is believed and intended. In some cases, the fussiness Castañeda or I might demand is just that; but in other cases—as we have just seen—it seems to matter.

agent, or even an agent other than myself. The precise description of this agent is a substantive matter in the content of the object of this attitude—the Castañedean topic of "guises." (We know this as well for legal and moral reasoning, since breaking a promise with a person with whom I know I have made a contract will be quite a different matter than not performing the promised activity for an arbitrary person.)

Consider this case: I may desire or wish that the fallen leaves not be in my lawn. Consequently, I may intend that I myself, an unspecified "someone," my wife, "the strongest person in the family" (which happens to be myself, unknown to me), or a hired neighbor boy get rid of them. (I may then generate various schemes for inducing agents to do this.) I may intend that someone *rake* them—i.e., a more precise specification of the means by which I see someone getting rid of them.[8] It is common to move from desired states (the leaves being gone) to proposed actions (someone raking them up), and the nexus has become so close for most cognitive agents that they are almost inseparable. I conjecture that desired (agentless) states are more fundamental, but that plans for bringing about desired states so routinely hinge on inducements to agents to bring them about that we begin to lose the distinction—i.e., a habit of planning leads us to move automatically from an observation ("The leaves cover the lawn and will kill the grass") to a proposed action ("Someone should rake the leaves") without specific, conscious reflection on the desired state, of leaflessness, that mediates the two.

Although this terminology distinguishes between "pro-attitudes"—Davidson's much-used term— toward "states" and toward "deeds," recent theories of action have shown a lack of appetite for debating whether there is a clear distinction, and whether one notion can and should be reduced to the other. Castañeda's efforts to argue for distinct cognitive objects of practical reasoning, which he calls "practitions," seem to presuppose a place for the distinction. [Castañeda, 1975]. My own earlier efforts to build computational models of agency that distinguish practitions from proposi- tions resulted in systems in which each half of the model was isomorphic to the other, save for tags of "propositional" and "practitional"; i.e., the two were functionally equivalent. Consequently I will not here place much weight either on the propositional/practitional distinction, nor on the older distinction between the "ought to be" *vs.* the "ought to do."[9]

I argue that the state of a cognitive agent that may rightfully be called an intention requires: (i) a genesis in a sequence of processes which I will broadly delineate as deliberation, planning, and decision, and (ii) that these processes be directed to data objects that have a certain fine structure. These processes and objects have an elaborate detail that I will characterize below, saying more

---

[8]I assume there exists a generic action-theoretic attitude toward representations of an agent together with an activity (these representations are roughly Castañeda's practitions). When the agent-representation is my self- representation, we usually call this an *intention*. That is, I admit we do not usually have "intentions" toward other agents. However, for convenience, I will use 'intention' both for this generic agent *cum* activity and for the more usual intention for oneself to do something.

[9]It is possible that Castañeda's distinction should be retained for reasons I do not now see, and which may or may not be "functionally" important. Aristotle seems to have employed a similar distinction between that which can be deliberated about and that which rationally cannot (i.e., facts), *Nic. Ethics* 1112a20f. D. Velleman has developed a suspiciously elaborate and reductionist account of how certain beliefs about one's future self can serve many of the roles intentions do [Brand *et al.* 1989]. The conceptual complexity of these beliefs seems, however, contrary to the more straightforward phenomenology of intentions.

about (i) than about (ii).[10] I take the generation of genuine intentions in an entity to be sufficient for agency, i.e. sufficient for the entity to constitute an agent; the question of what constitutes an *action* (and beyond that, of intentional *products*, i.e., artifacts and performances), or an actor, is a larger question involving issues of how these intentions causally or quasi-causally interact with non-cognitive tools, i.e. to body parts and the "external" world.

II

An account of deliberation is the core of my account. I assume that deliberation is typically initiated or triggered either by an earlier-formed intention, or by a desire or wish. The former case will be covered by planning, discussed below.

Once practical reasoning is initiated, one must then entertain or consider at least two actions, general courses of action, or states. They may be so rough-and-ready as "Someone raking the leaves" and "No one raking the leaves" (e.g., waiting for wind to blow them away). They may be so finely individuated as "Myself raking the leaves Tuesday afternoon with our old yellow rake," "Monika raking the leaves Wednesday with a new rake," etc. Consideration need not entail taking them as serious possibilities, but only in considering their relative merits. Aristotle in fact gives as incisive a summary as anyone has of the "particulars" by which contemplated actions may differ (*Nic. Ethics* 1111a3ff): agent, activity, object (e.g., direct object), instrument, goal and manner.[11] Deliberation is of course intuitively just a weighing of the advantages and disadvantages of the considered states or courses of action. However, simple *prudential* such consideration alone does not seem sufficient for the kind of deliberation required for agency (and subsequent decisions about responsibility). For example, if I, my dog, or a machine "considers" whether the pantry or the bookshelf is the best place to look for (fresh) food, it is hardly clear that such a conclusion based upon such simple decision-making is sufficient for agency. What is needed, I think we would want to say, is some consideration to the moral, not just the prudential, dimensions of actions—or at least an ability to do so. Strong evidence for this in ordinary usage comes from when individuals are "responsible" for actions, and specifically, the legal criterion of an ability to distinguish right from wrong. This seems to be one of the reasons why we would not consider one of the "planning" entities constructed in AI research to be an agent—even when the quantity or quality of ratiocination (although not yet the diversity) might exceed that of some human agents. (See [Christiansen 1985] and earlier work by E. Sacerdoti, Winograd, and others.) A description or simulation of rational planning is radically insufficient for agency and intention, even if it is in itself extremely difficult and worthwhile. To apply again the legal terminology, the entity must know the difference between right and wrong, and be capable of applying this distinction to contemplated actions.

The theory that best accommodates this observation is, I believe, the theory of "obligatoriness" operators proposed in [Castañeda 1975]. Castañeda seems to presuppose that genuine practical reasoning requires the contemplation of thoughts governed by "obligatoriness" operators, and that (i) they must include certain *kinds* of obligatoriness and (ii) the kinds of obligatoriness an agent

---

[10]This is so because I think the general framework of SNePS is adequate for, and in fact quite good at, capturing the salient, e.g., intensional, representational contours. Extensive and sophisticated work has been done within this framework on the best representation of all manner of difficult conceptual, perceptual, logical, and emotive notions.

[11]To be sure, each of these parameters may be complex. Also, we may have cognitive grounds for altering this list, perhaps even relative to the language—and hence favored conceptual scheme—of the actor.

employs must exhibit a certain minimal complexity. The deliberating agent has the attitude of belief toward these obligations. Although I will assume that the agent has "manifest," conscious beliefs toward various obligations, it is probably more common to have sketchy rules for generating obligations, and then generate them toward a given description of an activity upon demand. The difficulty here concerns the types of, and necessary and sufficient conditions for, believing.[12] His formal system implies that he considers the main objects of deliberation to be propositions (actually: more typically, practitions) governed by "obligatoriness" operators. These operators are indexed by their kind of obligatoriness. "Obligatoriness" should here be understood loosely, since what is indicated is not a specific moral value in contemplated actions, but any value in a proposed action whatsoever. Thus, Castañeda includes prudential obligatoriness, and this genus of obligatoriness may have its own species: according to physical laws, physical strength of human beings, and so on. Other genera of obligatoriness would include (separate) moral and legal operators. Legal notions themselves may have their own substructure: international, federal, state, county, city laws; college and department regulations; club rules etc. Moral obligatoriness might also have its species. We could also imagine the moral obligatoriness operator (or any other operator) being indexed by its reliability or security, and other epistemological indicators.[13]

The proposition governed by an obligatoriness operator may have its own logical structure. For example the formula:

$$obligated_{[promissorily, toBob, yesterday]} \text{ IF it rains,}$$
$$\text{THEN } I^* \text{ to drive Bob home.}$$

expresses the thought that (i) (I) am obligated by my promise, to Bob, yesterday that (ii) if it rains, then I myself am to drive him home. There is a great deal of complexity involving time, exact entities (Bob, home), and activity (drive) that is typically represented in the thought of an obligatory action, even if the verbal or diagrammatic representation of it is ambiguous or incomplete.

---

[12]About which, I might add, there is the same lack of detail as we see in action-theoretic attitudes. It is rather common to treat beliefs as if they were a very large stock of propositions located in an entity's cognitive apparatus. But most of our "beliefs"—the propositions we would assent to if presented with a formulation of them, and which would guide actions—are not *now* presently contemplated. Rather they are "implicit," or easily inferable (upon demand) from memories, active beliefs, and belief-formation rules. Neither, I think, is a remembered past belief necessarily a (present) "belief." Remembering that we once believed *p* may or may not, depending on our belief-formation apparatus, at the present point bring our assent to, or action upon, *p*. Most of the time it will, but this has less to do with the necessary nature of beliefs than with the inefficiency of constantly reconsidering (past) beliefs. We might say about repeatly contemplated, and assented-to propositions that there is not necessarily a present belief in them, but a *habit* of believing them when the occasion arises. Such propositions, actively believed, in the past then receive an interpretation much like the one I give below to "half-intention" actions: actions that are not fully consciously intended. I am generally quite dissatisfied with the existent philosophical accounts of beliefs and believing (but see [Price 1969]) and since so much in modern philosophy (e.g., definitions of knowledge and accounts of any ratiocination), and cognitive science relies on naive, even simple-minded assumptions about the nature of belief and believing, fear that these pursuits rest on shabby foundations.

[13]In the moral, and perhaps in other dimensions of obligation, we may have distinct evaluative operators, such as what is *permissible*, P for short, what is *forbidden*, F for short, as well as what is obligatory, O. These are in fact interreducible, although not necessarily actually interreduced in a given agent's conceptual scheme: 'F(X)' can be defined as 'O(not-X)' and 'P(X)' can be defined as 'not-F(X)'. For simplicity, I assume each dimension of obligatoriness has only one operator.

There have been extensive arguments offered in the literature for having such operators govern the whole conditional, rather than just the consequent, and I therefore regard this representational issue as settled [Castañeda 1975]. Prudential obligations, as we will see, are typically conditionals.[14]

Other than suggesting that things can get very complex, neither Castañeda nor, to my knowledge, anyone else has charted the main categories and sub-categories of obligatoriness. (An exception is [Castañeda 1982], which treats legal obligatoriness.) Although this may be important and useful for exploring the theory I am proposing, for our purposes here we face only three main questions: (1) What types of obligatoriness must be capable of being considered for an entity to be an agent? (2) Is there a minimum complexity to the structure of obligatoriness categories that an entity must possess in order to be an agent? and (3) What mechanisms must be present to weigh competing obligation-claims?

I have already argued that an ability to consider prudential obligations alone does not seem sufficient for agency. I would also argue that an ability to consider legal, promissory, and other "institutional" kinds of obligatoriness are also neither singly nor jointly sufficient for agency. This leaves, of course, the case that the presence in the entity's conceptual scheme of one or more kinds of moral obligatoriness is necessary for agency. But what is distinctive to a kind of obligatoriness being *moral* in an agent's thought? There is a temptation simply to think that labeling it "moral" in a diagram or knowledge representation scheme (e.g., an arc or case-frame in SNePS, or another semantic network system—see [McDermott 1981]) and saying it is "required" suffices. But it certainly doesn't. Since what it is to be morally obligatory plays an important role in our functional analysis of agency, we must say something about the *functional* role played by moral obligatoriness. What is required in the conceptual scheme of the entity—how must it function—for us justifiably to identify an obligatoriness as moral? This is a central issue in the history of philosophy (although not usually expressed in the way I have), and my tentative proposals say nothing new. I might suggest that there are at least two features about a kind or genus of obligatoriness that makes it moral: (A) It "trumps" other kinds of obligatoriness in the idealized version of the decision mechanism the agent employs (this mechanism is discussed below; see also [Castañeda 1974]), and (B) the obligatoriness is universalized on all objects in the agent's cognitive space that are themselves represented as agents. In other words, it has internal practitional priority as well as generality across other represented thought objects of a certain sort. As astutely noted in [Nussbaum 1986: 4-5], the view that there is a distinct *moral* value of actions, distinct from prudential, legal, aesthetic, or other values, is a modern view typical of Kant and after. We may then consider a conception of moral obligatoriness "modern" if it has both (A) and (B), and "classical" if it has only (B). It is usual, I think, for finite, human agents to have kinds of obligatoriness that are not (yet) "distilled" down to only one kind of moral obligatoriness. In these typical cases, (A) would have some force.

The second condition, (B), is more problematic. First, it might seem trivially satisfied by

---

[14]To an extent, what I have done in representing a basic "promissory" genus of obligatoriness is not an especially happy formulation. Whether and when one keeps promises may be for some individuals not an independent obligation-dimension, but reducible to prudential, moral, or even strictly legal obligatoriness. Exactly how, in a given agent, the major dimensions of obligatoriness are individuated is, for our concerns, less an issue than that they frequently are individuated. For many individuals, we might say, promise-keeping has not been reduced to a moral or legal matter. We could even regard the elusive ideal ethical man as having but one dimension of obligatoriness, namely, the moral, to which even the legal and prudential are reduced.

solipsism: I believe I am the only agent. However, the agents we contemplate are not restricted to the actual ones; we might guess then that to be an agent, an entity must contemplate other objects that it *considers*—fictionally or "really"—agents and to which this kind of obligatoriness applies.[15] Second, I find myself in the position of saying that agency definitionally requires a certain kind of deliberation among obligations and that among these obligation-beliefs are beliefs concerning other "agents"! I do not think this is such a serious problem as it might at first glance seem to be. I remark upon it merely to show I am not unaware of what is, I think, a non-vicious circularity, and one that correctly mirrors our own complex assumptions in this matter (e.g., the concept of agency involves the awareness of other agents).

Although I think that representations of moral obligatoriness are necessary for agency—perhaps alone necessary—I suspect that representations of prudential, moral, and legal[16] obligatoriness are typical of human thought. Some minds may have reduced these categories. Indeed, some human beings may have only legal and prudential categories, and may even have reduced the legal to the prudential. In my terminology they cease thereby to be genuine agents, although there may be various reasons in ethics and social policy to give entities that in fact might lack the strict form of agency an honorific status.[17] Epistemological problems of not knowing for certain that an entity is *not* an agent in this robust sense, and the dangers of treating an agent as a non-agent, are among the most serious of these considerations.

The Mechanisms of Deliberation. Once two obligations are contemplated, what does an agent do with them? We can conjecture that there are four dimensions to the process, and that their implementation in a computational system would involve an algorithm.[18] (i) First, the obligatory actions under a description are directly compared. We can imagine some internal prioritizing of types of obligation—an ordering of the indices of the obligatoriness operator or inferential rules governing governing them, based on the content of the proposition to which the operator is applied. Promises to friends take precedence over promises to others; the legal takes precedence over the

---

[15]It may not be necessary that I "actively" believe that every agent has such an obligation, but only that I have inferential mechanisms that would bring me to believe it. There is a problem even here of translating moral obligations I believe I have into the "analogous" context of the represented agent. This may be simple is some cases and difficult in others (e.g., where contexts and indexicals are at work). The ability to attribute analogous moral obligations may also require myths about others' cognitive apparatus for which we have no evidence—e.g., assumptions of translatability.

[16]By *legal* obligatoriness I mean any completely society- or institution-bound rules and standards. The notion of legality will have its functional cash value in the conceptualization of an institution—collectives of past and present agents structured by certain constraints and processes. This is indeed what many primitive thinkers mean by "morality." A pure such case would be the mythical German citizen, who concerns himself neither with moral nor prudential considerations that, e.g., he should sweep the sidewalk in front of his house once a week. The fact that the origins of the rule were once prudential or moral is irrelevant to the question of the type of obligatoriness an individual conceives it as having; there is a broader question of quasi-socio-historical or trans-individual agency that I here sidestep, instead choosing to explicate a "classical" Western notion of individual agency.

[17]We might call a cognitive entity that has at least some representations of legal obligatoriness a *social* entity, or even a "social" agent. Human beings are typically both (moral) agents and social entities in this sense.

[18]Aristotle in the *Nic. Ethics* suggests we must contemplate two or more actions that differ in particulars; we first *deliberate* (1112a13f) and then *decide* (1111b5f). The processes involved in the implementation, or failure to implement, this decision are discussed less clearly under his treatment of "characters of virtue" (e.g., self-control through habituation at 1103a13f) and his long and difficult discussion of weakness of will (*akrāsia* 1145b22ff).

prudential (or is it *vice versa?*), and so on. We have already mentioned the *a priori* requirement that all kinds of moral obligatoriness take precedence over any other kind. How complete is our ordering scheme? There are two questions here: (a) How much ordering must there be so that agency obtains? and (b) how much ordering is there in the typical human being? Other than the aforementioned requirement concerning moral obligatoriness, I do not see why an agent's scheme of obligatoriness operators (and other rules) could not be largely unprioritized. But it is quite clear that dilemmas would then be frequent, so I would guess that various rational maxims and bits of folk wisdom come to prioritize cross-genus comparisons of obligatoriness, and within major sub-genera—e.g., prudential over social etiquette (a "legal" obligatoriness in my classification). Within one genus, and especially within one species, dilemmas will nevertheless obtain.

(ii) Second, the obligatoriness of the two deeds under extensionally equivalent descriptions should be considered. After all, (to modify Davidson's famous example) my "flipping that little switch" may be known to be extensionally equivalent to electrocuting my best friend, or to be equivalent to beginning a nice surprise birthday party for my son. It is nevertheless surely too much to require that an agent compare two or more contemplated actions under all possible descriptions. But there are some cognitive maxims to limit the search, and they must be employed: e.g., the destruction of rocks is less likely to generate interesting kinds of obligatoriness than is the destruction of people or other animate objects. Not only are some known or knowable equivalent descriptions examined, but there may be an effort to investigate more unusual connections; this merges with the separate discussion of the required contemplation of consequences and side effects discussed below. (When I consider striking "that object, there"—which turns out to be someone's head—do we have a case of events under two descriptions, "hitting a dark object" vs. "hitting someone's head" or a cause-effect relation between my striking that object and someone's head hurting?)

(iii) Third, an agent must have the ability to consider the obligatoriness of causal consequences and side-effects of the contemplated actions. I stress the need for an ability to do so, rather than require that it be done. Since the typical human agent may have a vast amount of semi-reliable information that creates possible distant effects (e.g., the legendary calculations of the good, knowledgable utilitarian), it cannot be required, either for agency or for morality, that the agent actually do this calculation for all foreseeable effects. It is typical, one would guess, that human beings do calculate these effects to a certain causal distance, or along paths governed by certain considerations (e.g., probable effects on friends and others metaphysically "near" to them).[19]

(iv) Fourth—and this prefigures a discussion of planning in the next section—a rational agent must have the ability to calculate the merit of necessary means to achieve the contemplated actions. This merit would be established by applying i–iii to any state or action deemed necessary for the accomplishment of the main contemplated state or action. A further step would require the ability to assess the practitional merit of seriously contemplated jointly sufficient packages of means.

Finally, an agent must have some mechanism for summing weak or epistemological uncertain conclusions from i-iv above. I have assumed above that the process would be halted, or force backtracking, when a defeater is encountered; i.e., a clearly forbidden entailment in a high-priority form of obligatoriness. But since the kind of negative obligatoriness (i.e., forbidden-ness) may be

---

[19]For a discussion of ethics and the requirement of metaphysical "nearness" see [Dipert 1983], [Belliotti 1986], [Dipert 1990].

weak, or a low epistemological assessment may diminish its weight, an agent must have some ability to sum these accumulations that result from other than clear defeaters.

Also required for, or at least typical of human agency is, I suspect, an ability to deal with the situation in which all considered paths encounter defeaters or highly negative sums. The agent must then have the ability, first, to consider additional alternative main states or actions and, where this fails—i.e., in the case of genuine dilemmas—to continue deliberation beyond the encounter with normal defeaters and weigh negative sums. How extensively or well the agent does this is not an issue about agency itself. Aristotle at one point indicates that deliberation is always about "means," and never ends. What he precisely meant is one issue: he might have meant that the rational *final* unsubordinated end, i.e., his *eudaimonia*, is not to be retracted or reconsidered if all the means to it are unpleasant, or he might have meant that reconsideration of an end in such a case is not properly called 'deliberation.' (We have to remember that a "means" in one level of planning will be considered an "end" at a more detailed level of planning; so the notion of an 'end' is relative to a position in a menas-end hierarchy, and presumably cannot be taken to mean written in stone.) My account of deliberation differs from an interpretation of Aristotle, and perhaps many paradigms of planning, in that an end—even a final end—is not completely fixed: when all means to accomplishing it are problematic, this may force reconsideration of the (description of the) end itself.[20] This model will then be the analogue in practical reasoning of belief- (or scientific-theory-) revision in which there are no completely stable beliefs. I suspect that an ability to reconsider some ends and basically stable beliefs is necessary for agency; the ability to consider many, or all, is characteristic of *good* agents.

III

Planning. The extensive and sophisticated discussions of planning in the recent literature of artificial intelligence turn out not to be as central to the issue of agency as one might hope. This is so, first, because as mentioned above, researchers have often been more interested in an output of rational or even ideal plans and behavior than in minimum conditions for agency. Second, and relatedly, many discussions of planning have sought to establish the foundations for ideal, complete planning paradigms (e.g., J. Allen's elegant mechanisms use time-constraint planning), rather than planning mechanisms as close as possible—psychologically and phenomenologically "realistic"—to human planning. Work by Sacerdoti and others seems closer to incorporating aspects of cognitive modeling but has still been undertaken in a context disconnected from the broader issues of agency and action in broader senses. This literature is nevertheless now so diverse, extensive, and sophisticated that I cannot here do justice to the proposals or details of planning mechanisms. I must instead content myself with general features that I think might be required for agency, or typical of human planning.

I have already suggested that there are in fact two points at which planning enters the theory of agency and action theory. First, the ability to contemplate the merit of contemplated states

---

[20]A paradigm of a successful planning system in AI seems to be one that "solves" diverse problems. A mark of *agency* might be a system that refuses to play the game at all—e.g., as an immoral waste of its cognitive abilities. It will not simply accept any goal or end that is fed into it. This has the deeper methodological problem—from the point of confirming the presence of agency—that the system might be "output recalcitrant," i.e., decide not to reveal a solution or otherwise communicate; when I receive a survey form whose goals or presuppositions seem dubious, I refuse to participate.

or actions requires the ability also to calculate the merit of necessary means required to achieve this goal. The discussion of "means" and especially "necessary" means is obviously an issue of planning—and is a reason why deliberation and planning cannot be conceived as chronologically distinct steps. Second and more obviously, planning is typically required for the execution of intended actions or goal-states—that is, for eventual *action*.

Some few intentions or goals are "immediately executable" in a sense that is intuitively clear: I can easily raise my hand or walk across the room in a sense in which I cannot, say, get our Academic Vice President to accept my proposals for computers on campus or write an essay I am satisfied with on action theory. The notion of what is "immediately executable" is in fact rather troublesome, and will be addressed later; intuitively, we have habitualized or otherwise stored plans that no longer require conscious creation or conscious attention to their details.

But when the intended or desired state or intention is not immediately executable, we will construct a plan: a specification, perhaps only in outline, of states or intentions that contribute to the fulfillment of this plan. These derived means-states and intentions may in turn require further planning, and so on, down to a level of immediately executable intentions.

In the easiest, and possibly rare, cases, an intended action is grasped by the planning mechanism together with a means-end statement with a conditional form. Thus, from a conclusion that it is all-things-considered, or what I shall term '*absolutely*', obligatory to get a loaf of bread—a cognitive state just short of a full-fledged "intention"—and from the conditional obligation of the prudential sort, "To get a loaf of bread, go to the grocery store," we might be led by this tentative planning to the action to go to the grocery. That is, from:

$$obligatory_{[absolute]} I^* \text{ to get a loaf of bread.}$$

and:

$$obligatory_{[prudential]} \text{ IF X to get a loaf of bread}$$
$$\text{THEN X to go to the grocery.}$$

we may derive the tentative obligation:

$$obligatory_{[absolute, prudential]} I^* \text{ to go to the grocery.}$$

Observe that I have allowed myself some inferential machinery, instantiating X to I^*. Observe also that the derived or planned cognitive object is considered a "tentative" obligation, and is tagged with the obligatoriness it has accumulated through its inferential path. An ability to keep track of some of these obligatoriness indices will be necessary for the deliberation discussed in the previous section.[21] Finally, observe that a means-end rule will typically be *prudential*, and conditional in form, having roughly the action-theoretic force: in order to achieve (**antecedent**) you might consider doing (**consequent**), or the non-action-theoretic cognitive content that achieving

---

[21] Namely, we may in deliberation need to compare the overall obligatoriness of two such lists. We might have a rule such as, "The obligatoriness of a list is identical to the weakest operator in the list." As was pointed out to me by S. Shapiro in conversation, it is not necessary that the agent actually retain all of these accumulating lists of obligatoriness (although my program does), but just that he be able to infer some (e.g., the weakest) or all of them when that is crucial in deliberation.

the (consequent) contributes to achieving the (antecedent). It may be non-prudential, and may be more logically complex than a simple conditional and may involve complicated bindings of variables. More significantly, the means-ends rule will probably involve a "tag" that is more specific than the kind of obligatoriness (here: prudential). I have in mind specification of whether the connection is considered necessary (together with the *reliability* of that assessment), co-necessary with other conditions, sufficient, co-sufficient, and so on. It might seem at first cleverer, in the case of the sufficient condition, for example, simply to reverse the direction of the conditional. I do not do so, however, because I think that considerations in realistically representing means–ends relationships have, in action-theoretic contexts, a priority over logical convenience and adequacy. Roughly, I believe we (practically) think in terms of means-ends cognitive objects, rather than material conditionals. Furthermore, I would argue we attach certain quantitative measures to the degree to which we believe a condition is, roughly, "necessary" or "sufficient," and this would create chaos if we use a representational system based on the material conditional.[22] In other words, I am suggesting that a more accurate (action-theoretic) representation of what I wrote above as:

$obligatory_{[prudential]}$ IF X to get a loaf of bread
           THEN X to go to the grocery.

is:

$obligatory_{[prudential|necessarily]}$ X to go to the grocery **CONTRIBUTES TO** X to get a loaf of bread.

(supposing here the agent believes that loaves of bread are *necessarily* obtained in grocery stores). There is here a good representational question whether 'necessarily' should attach to the obligatoriness operator, how, what further parameters it may have (e.g., sub-indices), or whether it should be a separate operator, or—less desirable I think—whether it should attach to the 'CONTRUBUTES TO' practitional connective (or even individuate many such connectives); I adopt the above system as "good enough" for my purposes here. It is easy to see, for example, that the assessment of practitional merit discussed in step (iv) of deliberation would then have ready access to the relevant "necessary" means to ends.

A great deal of more creative planning in human beings is however not simply the kind of modus ponens/instantiation I use above. It would involve, among other things, (i) complicated analogical matches of means-ends rules to contemplated ends (rather than simple pattern matching/instantiations), (ii) higher-level maxims and strategies for planning, and (iii) seeking out for early planning and deliberation chronologically earliest contributants (i.e., preconditions), assessing the the ability to satisfy concurrent necessary or jointly sufficient contributants, and so on. Another significant and little-noticed element of planning is what we might call "agent reasoning": the assignment of a kind of obligatoriness to an agent in the practical reasoner's conceptual scheme.

---

[22]A possibly decisive reason for not conflating means-ends relationships and material conditionals arises in the vicinity of the paradox of material implication. Going from "X contributes in a necessary way to B" to a representation as a material conditional, "If B then A" is fine, but the truth of the material conditional, "If 2 plus 2 equals 5, then I'll win the Nobel Prize in Physics next year" hardly supports the means-end statement that making "2 plus 2 equals 5" contributes (in a sufficient way!) to the goal of winning the Nobel Prize. At the very least, the means-end connective must behave like that of relevant entailment. But why assume it is propositional at all?

Most planning puzzles in the AI literature assume that the planning agent is the only agent available and knows this. Hence, every state which will not naturally occur must be *brought about* by the planning agent itself. But every wily human agent knows—recalling the scenario of raking the leaves discussed earlier—that there are other agents to whom we might assign an obligatoriness in our own conceptual scheme (and then persuade them that they are obligated, or otherwise bring their behavior about). In this sense, we can form intentions that *others* should perform activities. These immediately become intentions to induce the agent to believe that he is obligated to perform the activity (perhaps by a form of obligatoriness different from the one we assigned to him).

Although deliberation can be begun before a full plan is devised, some planning will take place as part of deliberation (iv). Conversely, once a full plan is devised, or just before parts of what is expected to be a completable plan are executed, more final deliberation must take place. Namely, we must assess the practitional merit of the (non-necessary) means now being considered seriously after output from planning, i.e. what were termed "tentative" obligations above. Since even absolute intentions are retractable (recalling the discussion of revising ends above), there may be degrees of absoluteness (stability) and tentativeness.

Penultimately, a contemplated action has passed through both the steps of deliberation and planning. At this point, Castañeda suggests that it becomes, not yet an intention, but rather an all-things-considered or "absolute" obligation. Intuitively, we have concluded that it the right or good thing to do—as nearly as we can determine. That is, our attitude is one of endorsing it, of believing it is all-things-considered obligatory. Nevertheless, Castañeda suggests that this cognitive attitude may fail to mature into a full-fledged intention. Castañeda's motivation is unclear, but I suspect he is concerned to allow for as many conceivable sorts of weakness of will as possible. More concretely, I conjecture that a cognitive agent might hold its own deliberative and planning mechanisms in such a low regard that although it *thinks* this action is desirable, doubts about the quality of this thought inhibits—maybe properly so—it from becoming a full-fledged intention. This action-paralysis may in some instances embody wisdom, or may be pathological. Finally, should the entity have a high enough opinion of its deliberative machinery, the all-things-considered obligation would graduate into being an intention. If the object of the intention is immediately executable, and the somewhat mysterious causal mechanisms connecting mind and body are in order, behavior will result, that is, an *action* (if the behavior is described in the cognitive terms that were in fact intended).[23]

Implementation. Fragments of the above-sketched theory have been implemented in a computer system using a Prolog version (PSNePS) of the powerful intensional knowledge representation and reasoning system, SNePS. The reason for wanting to have a computer model involves comparing the resulting performance with human practical reasoning. Given the complex interaction of the various parts of the system, and their interaction with intensional representation systems and inference mechanisms, it is far from obvious how the model would operate, and thus whether it is plausible to regard it as characterising a minimal agent or typically human practical reasoning. Such computer models essentially then allow testing of some aspects of a theory's philosophical adequacy. The

---

[23]Another form of weakness of will may intrude at this last nexus. Namely, bodily or unconscious constraints (phobias, inhibitions, bad habits such as chronic procrastination, all typically non-conceptualized) may leave the "good intentions" as just that.

working model to date is so small as to be relatively unrevealing, except on small points.[24]

The model that has been constructed lacks so many of the features that are identified above as necessary for agency that there is no temptation to regard the resulting entity as an agent. Furthermore, even if *all* of the features indicated as necessary above were correctly modeled, there is reason to believe that the system could still not reasonably be regarded as an agent. The problem is its cognitive weakness. An insufficient number of data objects (concepts, propositions, and rules such as means-ends connections) would render the "functions" of these entities much less specific and articulated than are normal human thoughts. The problem then is roughly the same as deciding whether children and even infants are "agents"—i.e., they are at best marginal or difficult cases. Second, pending realistic input in the form of sensation or ordinary-language input, there would remain an overly simple connection of the system to the external world. Judging the agency— or "understanding" and other cognitive properties—of entities radically unlike us in central ways, such as having different histories, education, and socialization, is a serious, and perhaps intractable, obstacle [Dipert 1989a]. Third, the planning and inference mechanisms were not sufficiently sophisticated (although the planning and coordinating mechanisms are perhaps now constructible, and powerful inferential tools are available in SNePS, specifically in SNeBR—for which see [Martins and Shapiro 1988]). We will perhaps then at best see a system realistically mimicking various aspects of agency.

IV

One problem that faces any theory of action and agency is to distinguish between a fully conscious intention (and action) and one which is *not* fully conscious but which is in fact more common and still considered an "action." I turn to this example because it is extremely important and shows, I think, the explanatory power of the theory sketched above. Brand distinguishes between "actions" and "intentional actions," the latter a proper subset of the former [Brand 1984]. My driving on the right-hand side of the road today was an action but not a fully conscious or intentional one—i.e., it was not explicitly deliberated upon, but I am "responsible" for it.

Let us call such unconscious actions *half-intentional*, and an action under a description which was indeed fully contemplated and deliberated upon a *fully-intentional* action. We presume that the two are mutually exclusive and exhaustive of the class of actions. Intuitively, a half-intentional action is a habit, and there is clearly an interesting distinction between a habit and an "automatic" bit of behavior; my regularly beating heart is not a "habit" of mine, for example.[25]

My conjecture about the definition of a half-intentional action is this. Behavior X (under a description) is half-intentional if and only if: (1) X is causally tied by certain mechanisms to a fully intentional action (e.g., my decision to drive to town), (2) I once deliberated upon and planned

---

[24]The above-noted symmetry between propositional and practitional representations led to dropping the distinction. Another interesting feature involved agent-reasoning. In a scenario involving driving to the grocery store in order to get some oranges, the system reasoned—to the surprise of the designer who at first thought it was an error—that an agent other than driver might usefully be induced to turn the ignition key of the car. (The context involved a large number of legal, moral and prudential constraints.) Many trivial systems assume only one agent to perform actions, but this system was designed to do a search of available agents to induce to perform tasks, which is more in tune with actual social settings of practical reasoning.

[25]The class of events for which an agent is *responsible* may be still wider than the class of that agent's actions, e.g., negligence or doctrines of strict liability.

doing X (with variations allowed only among times, and other small parameters), (3) the repeated execution of practical reasoning to do X in similar circumstances brought about direct causal-cognitive paths between the triggering, fully intentional actions and the resulting behavior, (4) I allowed or decided to let that connection become established, and (5) I could now deliberate about and perform X fully intentionally if I wished (or, therefore, deliberate about X and refuse to perform it).

Conditions (3) and (4) essentially give conditions on the kind of causal links between the triggering full intention discussed in (1). The account conforms well to the account of habituation in Aristotle's *Nichomachean Ethics*. It is fairly obvious I think that numerous acts of motor control (e.g., putting left foot in front of right when walking, or in even more motor detail) were once fully intentional, at least as far as our status as children qualified us as agents at all. Gradually, and clearly for reasons of efficiency, these came to be packaged in terms of sequences of motor control with conscious access primarily through high-level cognitive labels of these packages as routines, e.g., walking. We can see, definitionally, that no agent can produce only half-intentional actions. Condition (2) requires a past history of deliberation, and condition (1) requires causal chains beginning with present (or at least recent) full intentions.

As writers as diverse as Aristotle and Peirce emphasize, our behavior, even our thought, is primarily composed of such habits, and there is a *desideratum* of having the largest possible, regularly performed sequence of actions as habits. (Creative artists thus develop personal idioms or styles which are no longer explicitly contemplated before each work is created; there are similar habitual mechanisms that govern decisions about when to use keyboard "macros" in word-processing packages or other programs.) Contrary to the views we might gather from (casually) reading Kant and other ethicists, extreme, conscious deliberative control over all of our "actions" is neither desirable nor possible for finite creatures. The complexity of the deliberation mechanism we have sketched above, and the depth of some of the search trees (e.g., into side effects), show just how onerous this would be, especially to do it well. Control over the habituation mechanism itself—i.e., decisions to let something become or make it a habit—are probably where the most interesting ethical triumphs and failures occur (again, an observation going back to Aristotle), and not in constant, agonizing deliberation over highly particular actions. This is classically identified with "character" but is more than just dispositions to behave in a certain way. I should add that since reasoning and deliberating themselves are to a large extent under cognitive control, various inferences and observations may be fully intentional or half-intentional—and unfortunately often dominated by sloppy habits of thought.

This sketch of human agency must be taken as incomplete, or even as simply being a research proposal for a full such theory. Nevertheless, we can see in it a complexity that seems truer to the complexity and diversity of actual human action than is, say, a picture of a human being as simple pleasure maximizing creature, or of an entity that has fixed ends and rationally picks means. For one thing, an individual cognitive agent experiences the world in terms of subtly distinguished intensional "guises" to which even (especially?) language does not do justice. Second, the dimensions along which contemplated actions are measured are typically extraordinarily diverse and complex (prudential, legal, moral,... plus epistemological, confidence and risk measures)—and typically in ways that are not considered inter-reducible by the agent, perhaps for good reason. The simplistic caricature of a calculating "economic" man working with "beliefs" and "desires" that still occasionally dominates our picture of agency and practical reasoning appears grossly out of tune with the actual nature of human action, viewed either phenomenologically—internally as it were—or sociologically. This observation in turn raises the possibility that we could perhaps better model economic and other social behavior using computer models of whole "societies" of "agents" like the ones described above, by using much more refined notions of agency, and especially, of typically human agency.[26]

Bibliography

Aristotle, *Nicomachean Ethics* trans. by T. Irwin (Indianapolis: Hackett, 1985).

[Belliotti 1986] R. Belliotti, "Honor Thy Father and Thy Mother," *Southern Journal of Philosophy* 24 (1986): 149-162.

[Brachman and Levesque 1985] Brachman, Ronald J., and Levesque, Hector J. (eds.), *Readings in Knowledge Representation* (Los Altos, CA: Morgan Kaufmann, 1985).

[Brand 1984] M. Brand, *Intending and Acting: Toward a Naturalized Action Theory* (Cambridge, Mass.: MIT, 1984).

[Brand et al. 1989] M. Brand, chair; commentators D. Velleman and H. McCann; respondent M. Bratman, "Symposium on Michael Bratman's *Intentions, Plans and Practical Reason*," APA Central Division Meetings, Chicago, 1989.

[Bratman and Lansky 1986] M. Bratman and A. Lansky "Rational Agency (RatAg)," *CSLI Monthly* 1.4 (June 1986).

[Bratman 1987] M. Bratman, *Intention, Plans, and Practical Reason* (Cambridge, Mass.: Harvard, 1987).

[Castañeda 1974] H.-N. Castañeda, *The Structure of Morality* (Springfield, IL: Charles Thomas, 1974).

---

[26]This is developed in [Dipert 1987] and is a criticism of economic theories from Smith and Hume to von Hayek and von Mises.

[Castañeda 1975] H.-N. Castañeda, *Thinking and Doing* (Dordrecht, Holland: D. Reidel, 1975).

[Castañeda 1982] H.-N. Castañeda, "The Logical Structure of Legal Systems: A New Perspective," in A. Martino (ed.) *Deontic Logic, Computational Linguistics, and Legal Information Systems*, Vol. II (Dordrecht, Holland: North-Holland, 1982).

[Christiansen 1985] A.D. Christiansen, "The History of Planning Methodology: An Annotated Bibliography," *SIGART Newsletter*, No. 84 (October 1985), pp. 44f.

[Cohen and Levesque 1987] "Persistence, Intention, and Commitment," in [Georgeff and Lansky 1987].

[Dipert 1986] Randall R. Dipert, "Art, Artifacts, and Regarded Intentions," *American Philosophical Quarterly* 23 (1986): 401–408.

[Dipert 1987] R.R. Dipert, "Handlungstheorie, praktisches Denken und Computer: Reflexionen aus Philosophie, Wirtschaftstheorie, und künstlicher Intelligenz," Ludwig von Mises Privatseminar, organized by the Carl Menger Institut and held in the Wiener Handelskammer, Vienna, 1987.

[Dipert 1989a] "The Moon Box: Methodological Reflections on the Determination of the Presence of Understanding," unpublished paper delivered to the Buffalo Logic Colloquium, spring, 1989.

[Dipert 1990] *The Ethical Dimensions of Friendship: An Essay and Anthology* (manuscript).

[Georgeff and Lansky 1987] *Reasoning about Actions and Plans* (San Mateo, CA: Morgan Kaufmann, 1987).

[Haugeland 1981] John Haugeland (ed.), *Mind Design: Philosophy, Psychology, Artificial Intelligence* (Cambridge, MA: MIT Press, 1981).

[Maida and Shapiro 1982] Anthony S. Maida and Stuart C. Shapiro, "Intensional Concepts in Propositional Semantic Networks," *Cognitive Science* 6 (1982): 291-330; reprinted in [Brachman and Levesque 1985: 169-189].

[Martins and Shapiro 1988] Martins, João, and Shapiro, Stuart C., "A Model for Belief Revision," *Artificial Intelligence* 35 (1988): 25-79.

[McDermott 1981] Drew McDermott, "Artificial Intelligence Meets Natural Stupidity," in [Haugeland 1981: 143-160].

[Meinong 1907] Alexius Meinong, *Über die Stellung der Gegenstandstheorie im System der Wissenschaften* (1907).

[Nussbaum 1986] Martha Nussbaum, *The Fragility of Goodness* (New York: Cambridge University Press, 1986).

[Price 1969] H.H. Price, *Belief* (New York: Humanities Press, 1969).

[Putnam 1988] Hilary Putnam, *Representation and Reality* (Cambridge, Mass.: MIT Press, 1988).

[Rapaport, 1986] W. J. Rapaport, "Logical Foundations for Belief Representation," *Cognitive Science* 10 (1986) 371-422.

[Rapaport and Shapiro, 1987] W.J. Rapaport and S.C. Shapiro, "SNePS Considered as a Fully Intensional Propositional Semantic Network," in N. Cercone and G. McCalla (eds.), *The Knowledge Frontier: Essays in the Representation of Knowledge* (New York: Springer-Verlag): 262-315; earlier version preprinted as *Technical Report* No. 85-15 (Buffalo: SUNY Buffalo Department of Computer Science, 1985); shorter version appeared in *Proceedings of the Fifth National Conference on Artificial Intelligence* (AAAI-86, Philadelphia) (Los Altos, CA: Morgan Kaufmann): 278-283.

[Shapiro 1979] S. C. Shapiro, "The SNePS Semantic Network Processing System," in N.V. Findler (ed.) *Associative Networks* (New York: Academic Press, 1979): 179-203.

[Tomberlin 1986] J.E. Tomberlin, *Hector-Neri Castañeda* (Dordrecht, Holland: D. Reidel, 1986).

[Wilkins 1988] David Wilkins, *Practical Planning: Extending the Classical AI Planning Paradigm* (San Mateo, CA: Morgan Kaufmann, 1988).

Combining Linguistic and Pictorial Information: Using Captions to Interpret Newspaper Photographs

Rohini K. Srihari and William J. Rapaport
Department of Computer Science
State University of New York at Buffalo
Buffalo, New York 14260 USA
srihari, rapaport@cs.buffalo.edu

Abstract

There are many situations where linguistic and pictorial data are jointly presented to communicate information. A computer model for synthesising information from the two sources requires an initial interpretation of both the text and the picture followed by consolidation of information. The problem of performing general-purpose vision (without apriori knowledge) would make this a nearly impossible task. However, in some situations, the text describes salient aspects of the picture. In such situations, it is possible to extract visual information from the text, resulting in a relational graph describing the structure of the accompanying picture. This graph can then be used by a computer vision system to guide the interpretation of the picture. This paper discusses an application whereby information obtained from parsing a caption of a newspaper photograph is used to identify human faces in the photograph. Heuristics are described for extracting information from the caption which contributes to the hypothesised structure of the picture. The top-down processing of the image using this information is discussed.

1 Introduction

There are many situations where words and pictures are combined to form a communicative unit; examples in the print media include pictures with captions, annotated diagrams, and weather charts. In order for a computer system to synthesise the information from these two diverse sources of information, it is necessary to perform the preliminary operations of natural-language processing of the text and image interpretation of the associated picture. This would result in an initial interpretation of the text and image, following which an attempt at consolidation of the information could be made. Although vision and natural-language processing are challenging tasks, since they are severely under-constrained, natural-language processing can more easily exploit constraints posed by the syntax of the language than vision systems can exploit constraints about the physical world. This fact, combined with the observation that the text often describes salient features of the accompanying picture in joint communicative units, leads to the idea of using the information contained in the text as a guide to interpreting the picture. This paper focuses on a method of extracting visual information from text, which results in a relational graph describing the hypothesised structure of the accompanying picture (in terms of the objects present and their spatial relationships). The relational graph is subsequently used by a vision system to guide the interpretation of the picture. We describe the implementation of a system which labels human faces in a newspaper photograph, based on information obtained from parsing the caption. A common representation, namely a semantic network, is used for the knowledge contained in both the picture and the caption. The theory is general enough to permit construction of a picture when given arbitrary descriptive text (without an accompanying picture).

Newspaper photographs have all the elements required for a true integration of linguistic and visual information. Accompanying captions usually identify objects and provide background information which the photograph alone cannot. Photographs, on the other hand, provide visual detail which the captions do not. Newspaper captions often identify people in a picture through visual detail such as "Tom Jones, wearing sunglasses ...". In order for a computer system to be able to identify Tom Jones, it is necessary to understand the visual implication of the phrase "wearing sunglasses". The face satisfying all the implied visual constraints could then be labeled accordingly.

The idea of integrating natural language and vision has been relatively unexplored. [AST81, YTK84] are two systems which consider the bidirectional flow of control from text to a related picture and vice versa. Several systems have implemented a portion of the task. Generating natural-language descriptions of results obtained from a vision system is considered in [MP87, NN83]. The reverse process of generating pictures based on natural-language input is considered in [AMG84, WB79]. [Her86] discusses a theory of encoding and decoding English expressions of location, which focuses on the meaning of prepositional phrases. In the research being presented here, the emphasis is on generating a description of a picture (rather than a picture itself), such that the description can be used by a vision system to actually find the required objects and relationships in an associated picture. [ZV88] attempts a similar task when given locative expressions pertaining to airport scenes.

This paper describes a three-stage process used to identify human faces in newspaper photographs. We consider only those photographs whose captions are factual but sometimes incomplete in their description of the photograph. In the first stage, information pertaining to the story is extracted from the caption, and a structure of the picture in terms of the objects present and spatial relationships between them is predicted. The information contained in this structure would be sufficient for generating a picture representing the meaning of the caption. Using this information to label faces in an existing picture however, entails further processing. The second stage which constitutes the vision component, calls on a procedure to locate human faces in photographs when the number of faces and their approximate sizes are known. Although the second stage locates faces, it does not know whose they are. The last stage establishes a unique correlation between names mentioned in the caption and their corresponding areas in the image. These associations are recorded in a semantic network and enable us to selectively view human faces as well as obtain information about them. Input to the system is a digitized image of a newspaper photograph with a caption, as in Figure 1. The system returns a labeling of parts of the image corresponding to the faces of the people mentioned in the caption, as in Figures 2a, b, c and d. [SR89] describes earlier work on this project.

Figure 1: *A newspaper photograph with caption "Wearing their new Celtics sunglasses are Joseph Crowley, standing with pennant, and seated from left, Paul Cotter, John Webb and David Buck."*

2 Processing The Caption

The process of interpreting the caption has two main goals. The first is the representation of the factual information contained in the caption. This is explicit information provided by the caption, namely the identification of the people in the photograph and the context under which the photograph was taken. More important for our application, however, is the second goal, the construction of a relational graph representing the expected structure of the picture. The relational graph includes information such as the objects hypothesised to be in the picture, their physical appearance. and spatial relationships between them. This is similar to dynamic schema construction [Wey86]. We use the SNePS knowledge-representation and reasoning system to represent both factual information and the relational graph derived from the caption [SR87]. A common representation

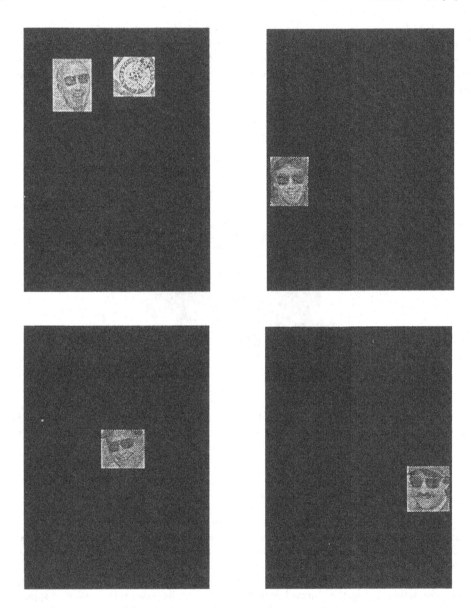

Figure 2: *(a) output of system when asked to display Joseph Crowley (b) output of system when asked to display Paul Cotter (c) output of system when asked to display John Webb (d) output of system when asked to display David Buck*

facilitates the integration of information from both sources. SNePS is a fully intensional, propositional, semantic-network processing system in which every node represents a unique concept. It can perform node-based and path-based inference [Sri81], and it also provides a natural-language parsing and generating facility [Sha82].

Figure 3 illustrates the partial output of the parser on the caption of Figure 1. It postulates that four humans, namely Joseph Crowley, Paul Cotter, John Webb and David Buck are present in the picture (nodes m38, m42, m46 and m50). Furthermore, it postulates that Joseph Crowley appears above the other three in the picture (since he is "standing") as represented by nodes m51, m52 and m53. The left to right ordering of the remaining three members is represented by the "left-of" relationship in nodes m54 and m55. Factual information obtained from the caption (m31) is separated from derived visual information (b12). The hypothesised presence of an object in the picture is represented by a node (e.g. m38) with three arcs: COLLECTION, referring to the visual model it is part of; TYPE indicating whether the object is explicitly mentioned in the caption or inferred to be present; and MEMBER pointing to a detailed model of this object (e.g. b10). A node such as m37 provides the link between the visual model of an object and the proper name it is associated with (in this case Paul Cotter). Hypothesised spatial relations between objects are represented by a node (e.g. m52) with 3 arcs pointing to (a) the type of spatial relation and (b) the nodes representing the two arguments to this binary relation.

2.1   Predicting Objects

There are three classes of heuristics used to extract information from the caption: rules that predict the presence of objects, rules that predict spatial relations between objects and rules that predict configurations of objects. Depending on the type of sentence, several rules are used to predict the presence of objects in a picture. We have observed that many captions are of the form "<subject list> <prepositional-phrase list>". A <prepositional-phrase list> is a series of preposition + noun-phrase pairs, as in the caption of Figure 1a. In such sentences, we propose that each of the subjects in <subject list> is present in the picture. We can judge whether the entire object is present in the picture based on its scale. We carefully avoid predicting objects which are mentioned in the caption but are not present in the picture. In many phrases of the form "<subject> <verb-phrase> <direct-object>", the verb-phrase (e.g., wearing, holding, greeting) indicates the presence of the direct object in the picture. The notion of time is very important here. Captions are traditionally in the present tense even though they refer to events in the past. We have observed that any object referred to at a time previous to the current time is not in the picture.

We also stress the importance of correctly predicting the class of an object. A recent photograph in *The Buffalo News* depicted a horse and her trainer. The caption was "Winning Colors being grazed by her trainer, Wayne Lucas, yesterday morning before the running of the Kentucky Derby". A simplistic parser might conclude that the name "Winning Colors" referred to a human, based on the fact that it was a sequence of two capitalized words serving the subject role in a sentence. This would predict the presence of two human faces and thus provide incorrect data to the face-location module. A more sophisticated parser would realise that the object of "grazing" is usually an animal such as a cow or a horse. If the parser had access to information about the Kentucky Derby, it

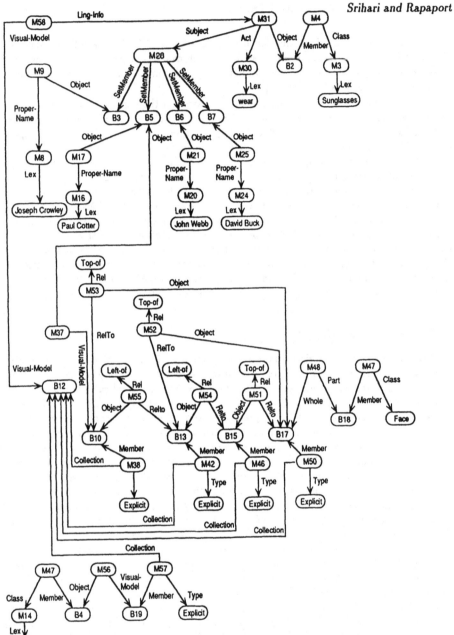

Figure 3: *Partial output of the parser on caption of Figure 1*

could conclude definitely that "Winning Colors" was a horse. If this information were not known, the vision component of the system would be called on to disambiguate between the possibilities of a horse and cow. The last case illustrates the bi-directional flow of information from the caption to the picture and vice versa.

2.2 Predicting Spatial Relations Between Objects

Specifying spatial relations between objects is the principal method of identification. The caption often explicitly specifies the spatial relation, as in "Thomas Walker, left, John Roberts, center ..." thus making the task relatively simple. However, it is not as simple in the case of captions which combine implicit and explicit means of identification. Consider the caption "The All-WNY boys volleyball team surrounds the coach of the year, Frontier's Kevin Starr. Top row, from left, are ..." accompanying a group photograph. The spatial location of the coach must be inferred first through a detailed understanding of the word *surrounds*. The row and column relationships can then be correctly interpreted. Such examples provide are providing a real challenge to both the language-parsing as well as the face-locating stages of our system.

An implicit method of identification frequently used is the ordering of the subjects in the caption to reflect their order in the picture. Our grammar has been designed to assert the spatial relation *left-of* when parsing a list of subjects. There is frequent departure from the above convention in pictures depicting well-known subjects or in male-female pairs since it is assumed that the reader can disambiguate. In such cases, the grammar asserts the relationship "adjacent", indicating further evidence is required before identification can be made. The labeling procedure uses world knowledge (such as relative heights) to establish a unique correlation between names mentioned in the caption and faces located in the photograph. Many captions combine implicit and explicit means of identification such as "Mayor Coleman Young of Detroit, right, with Michael Ilitch and his wife at a dinner last week". The system is able to handle such cases correctly.

2.3 Predicting Configurations of Objects

The model description for a class of objects contains a description of a prototype for that class. In the absence of any further information, only the default portions of the model will be instantiated. However, there is often detailed information in the caption pertaining to the specific configuration of an object, which can be represented by instantiating optional components (or configurations) in the model description of the particular object. Some caption types use such visual detail in order to uniquely identify people (or other objects). For instance, consider the caption "Thomas Smith, wearing dark tophat, and Richard Jones, ...". Processing this example would require instantiating the visual model of a person wearing a tophat. Since we cannot possibly have previously stored visual models of all such configurations, the visual model must be constructed dynamically when parsing. It would be necessary to associate visual information with the word "tophat" such that the event "wearing tophat" would cause the instantiation of a visual model with the desired spatial relationships between the wearer and the tophat. It should be noted that a high degree of inter-connection between the two objects (relationships between the parts of one object and the parts of another) dramatically increases the complexity of constructing a viable visual model. The objective is to construct the least complex visual model which will suffice for identification purposes. This is currently being investigated.

There is far more visual information which can be derived from text if we are not restricted to simply the task of identification. A simple example of this is the use of words such as "sitting" or "standing" which express different configurations of human body parts. The phrase "shaking hands with" implies a configuration of the arms perpendicular to the body, and the hands of the individuals touching. Consider a caption which refers to a baseball player "diving" for a ball. The use of the word "dive" along with the context of baseball suggest a more horizontal configuration of the body. This information can be valuable if it becomes necessary to detect the entire body (torso, legs etc.), rather than just the face. Jackendoff [Jac87] summarises this idea by saying that many verbs of station and locomotion are used more to express 3D configurations of objects than to express action.

3   Processing The Picture

Picture processing in this project is the process of using the information in the hypothesised structure to find relevant objects and spatial relationships in the picture. Currently, we only deal with human faces. Since the caption often gives us spatial constraints on the location of objects, it is frequently sufficient to use crude object-detection modules. In this application, we use a face-locator module which generates candidates for faces. It is often the case that spatial constraints alone are sufficient for eliminating false candidates.

Using caption information and heuristics from photojournalism [Arn69], the possible range of face sizes appearing in a newspaper photograph can be narrowed. ¿From the caption, we are able to determine the number of faces and some weak bounds on the size of faces. These constitute parameters to the face-location module, which works in three stages: feature selection, feature detection, and grouping. We have selected as features the two arcs corresponding to the hair-line and the chin-line, and the two lines corresponding to the sides of the face. These features seem to be robust, since they are not greatly affected by factors such as scale, viewing position, or resolution. Furthermore, they are relatively easy to detect. A first-level Hough transform detects the arcs and collinear edge-elements in the image. A line-finder then uses back-projection from the accumulator array to the original image to extract line segments. The curves and line segments are grouped together by a modified Hough transform to generate candidate regions for locations of faces [GSSS89]. The generated candidates are then refined using filters such as pixel-ratios and symmetries. The final output of the face locator on the image of Figure 1 is shown in Figure 4.

For each image area hypothesised to be a face, this module returns the coordinates of a bounding rectangle for that area. This facilitates the representation of image data in the semantic network.

Figure 4: *Face candidates remaining after filtering*

4   Constraint Satisfaction

In general, the location procedure generates more candidates than required (Figure 4). We have already shown how linguistic heuristics can be used to derive spatial constraints from the caption when they are not explicitly given. These constraints are applied to the candidates generated by the face-locator to produce all possible *bindings*. A labeling algorithm [HS79] is employed which uses a look-ahead operator in order to eliminate backtracking in the treesearch. If $C = c_1 \ldots c_j$ represent candidates generated by the face-finder and $N = b_1 \ldots b_k$ are SNePS nodes representing the people predicted to be in the picture, then a binding B, is defined as the set of tuples $B = \{B_i\}_{i=1}^{k}$, where $B_i = (b_i, c_{x_i})$ such that $c_x \epsilon C$ and $\forall i = 1 \ldots k$, if $m \neq n$ then $c_{x_m} \neq c_{x_n}$. A "binding" represents the assignment of correspondence between face candidates and people predicted to be in the picture.

5   Refining Candidates and Labeling Faces

Because a large number of candidates are generated by the face-locator, spatial constraints alone cannot produce a unique binding between candidates and people mentioned in the caption. Furthermore, a spatial constraint such as "adjacent" (used frequently in male-female pairs) will produce at least two possibilities. What is essentially needed, is a method of evaluating the bindings produced by the constraint satisfier and selecting the best one(s). This is the purpose of the refinement and identification module.

We refer to each of the tuples in a binding as a "match". The refinement and identification rules fall into three categories: a) those that update the confidence of a candidate being a face (irrespective of which person that face is associated with), b) those that update the confidence of a "match", i.e. the confidence that a particular face candidate corresponds to a named person and c) those that update the confidence of an entire binding. Refinement rules are used to weed out poor candidates whereas identification rules are used for labeling. Even in cases where exactly the required number of faces are obtained, labeling may entail further processing. An example of a refinement rule of type (a) is one that examines the centrality of the face candidate in the image. This rule weakens the confidence of face candidates which appear near the edges of the image. An example of a refinement rule of type (b) is one which takes into account the face size. The face locator returns a variety of face sizes. An examination of several pictures revealed that faces in the background of a picture (not explicitly mentioned in the caption) tended to be smaller than those in the foreground. The rule checks for this condition in matches where the face corresponds to an adult. An example of a refinement rule in the last category is one which examines height relationships between people in the same row. It favours those bindings where the vertical positions of faces do not differ significantly.

The system does not have any identification rules of type (a) since identification is not possible unless you know which person is being identified. Identification rules of type (b) are those which use image intrinsic features particular to a certain person (e.g. baldness, short vs. tall etc.). Finally, an example of a binding identification rule is one which examines the relative heights between members of a binding and checks whether the males are taller than the females.

A technique was required in order to combine the evidence that each rule provides towards some hypothesis. Currently, we are experimenting with a modified Bayesian updating scheme. Assuming that we are able to generate the three types of confidences described above, the weight of a match, $weight_{match_i}$ is computed as $confidence_{c_si} * confidence_{match_i}$. We assign a weight W to every binding B, such that $W = [\prod_{i=1}^{k} weight_{match_i}] * confidence_B$ where $confidence_B$ is the confidence associated with the binding itself. If the weight of bindings differ by less than a preset threshold, $thresh_1$, then they are considered equivalent. This creates multiple correspondences for some or all of the faces. Labeling information is represented in the semantic network by asserting nodes which associate concepts of people with the corresponding areas in the image. In cases where the system cannot uniquely identify faces, all possible candidates for each person appearing in the caption are recorded.

6   Summary

Our system for understanding newspaper pictures with captions consists of a three-stage process whereby the caption is first parsed with the goal of predicting the structure of the picture. The second stage uses information from the first stage in a top-down processing of the image. The final stage, labeling, is the process of matching pictures of objects with the words representing them in the caption.

The next step in this research is generating visual models for expressions containing certain verb phrases which have a similar visual implication to everyone (e.g. wearing hat, shaking hands). Such phrases are frequently used in captions to identify people in the photograph.

This work was supported by National Science Foundation grants IRI-8613361 and IRI-8610517.

References

[AMG84] Giovanni Adorni, Mauro Di Manzo, and Fausto Giunchiglia. Natural Language Driven Image Generation. In *Proceedings of COLING*, pages 495–500, 1984.

[Arn69] Edmund C. Arnold. *Modern Newspaper Design*. Harper and Row, New York, NY, 1969.

[AST81] N. Abe, I. Soga, and S. Tsuji. A Plot Understanding System on Reference to Both Image and Language. In *Proceedings of IJCAI*, pages 77–84, 1981.

[GSSS89] Venu Govindaraju, David B. Sher, Rohini K. Srihari, and Sargur N. Srihari. Locating human faces in newspaper photographs. In *Proceedings of CVPR*, pages 549–554, 1989.

[Her86] Annette Herskovits. *Language and Spatial Cognition*. Cambridge University Press, 1986.

[HS79] Robert M. Haralick and Linda G. Shapiro. The Consistent Labeling Problem: Part 1. *IEEE Transactions on Pattern Analysis and Machine Intelligence*, PAMI-1(2):173–184, 1979.

[Jac87] Ray Jackendoff. On Beyond Zebra: The Relation of Linguistic and Visual Information. *Cognition*, 26(2):89–114, 1987.

[MP87] Anthony B. Maddox and James Pustejovsky. Linguistic Descriptions of Visual Event Perceptions. In *Proceedings of the Cognitive Science Society Conference*, pages 442–454, Seattle, 1987.

[NN83] B. Neumann and H. Novak. Event Models for Recognition and Natural Language Description of Events in Real-World Image Sequences. In *Proceedings of IJCAI 1983*, pages 724–726, 1983.

[Sha82] Stuart C. Shapiro. Generalized Augmented Transition Network Grammars for Generation from Semantic Networks. *The American Journal for Computational Linguistics*, 8(2):12–25, 1982.

[SR87] Stuart C. Shapiro and William J. Rapaport. SNePS Considered as a Fully Intensional Propositional Semantic Network. In Nick Cercone and Gordon McCalla, editors, *The Knowledge Frontier, Essays in the Representation of Knowledge*, pages 262–315. Springer-Verlag, New York, 1987.

[SR89]   Rohini K. Srihari and William J. Rapaport. Extracting Visual Information From Text:
          Using Captions to Label Human Faces in Newspaper Photographs. In *Proceedings of
          the 11th Annual Conference of the Cognitive Society*, pages 364–371. Lawrence Erlbaum
          Associates, 1989.

[Sri81]   Rohini K. Srihari. Combining Path-based and Node-based Reasoning in SNePS. Technical
          Report 183, SUNY at Buffalo, 1981.

[WB79]   David L. Waltz and L. Boggess. Visual Analog Representation for Natural Language
          Understanding. In *Proceedings of IJCAI*, pages 926–934, 1979.

[Wey86]   T.E. Weymouth. *Using Object Descriptions in a Schema Network for Machine Vision*.
          PhD thesis, University of Masschussetts at Amherst, 1986.

[YTK84]   Masao Yokota, Rin-ichiro Taniguchi, and Eiji Kawaguchi. Language-Picture Question-
          Answering Through Common Semantic Representation and its Application to the World
          of Weather Report. In Leonard Bolc, editor, *Natural Language Communication with
          Pictorial Information Systems*. Springer-Verlag, 1984.

[ZV88]   Uri Zernik and Barbara J. Vivier. How Near Is Too Far? Talking about Visual Images.
          In *Proceedings of the Tenth Annual Conference of the Cognitive Science Society*, pages
          202–208. Lawrence Erlbaum Associates, 1988.

Knowledge Based Lexicons

J. Terry Nutter*
Virginia Polytechnic Institute and State University
Blacksburg, Virginia 24061
nutter@vtopus.cs.vt.edu

Abstract

To date, most lexicons for AI systems contain essentially syntactic information, with some minimal semantic information, usually in the form of property flags to help with selection restrictions. Any further semantic information usually has entirely separate representations elsewhere. As a rule, semantic information looks like any other knowledge in the system's knowledge base: that is, it appears as knowledge about the world, not as knowledge about words. But increasingly systems need to know about words to operate effectively. This report deals with a new unified representation for lexical information.

1 Introduction

AI systems which involve natural language usually have at least three different knowledge bases: one for domain information, one for language rules, and one for information about words. Especially in comparison with domain information, knowledge about words tends to be isolated, fragmented, and impoverished. It is isolated, in that much of the information lies in specialized structures to which the system's reasoning mechanisms have little or no access, and which must be manipulated by specialized (and usually very limited) algorithms. It is fragmented, in that most on-line lexicons represent primarily syntactic information. Semantic information, when it is present at all, is usually in a separate representation scheme, accessible by different techniques. Information which requires both syntax and semantics for its representation usually falls through the cracks, as does information which is at least in part semantic, but which is less about the world than about the words. It is impoverished, in that all kinds of information tend to be represented sketchily, with little apparent concern for giving systems the kinds of information about words to which humans have routine access.

Few people would argue for impoverished representations in the long run; they have lasted this long primarily because attention has lain elsewhere. But isolation and fragmentation are also serious problems. There is good reason to believe that segregating information about words from domain

---

*This research was supported in part by the National Science Foundation under grant IRI-8703580.

information is far from optimal, in that there seems to be no hard and fast line between dictionary meanings and encyclopedic information, with which semantic information must at least interact if it is to be used effectively. Similar remarks hold for separating semantic from syntactic information. Research in linguistics supports the view that even at the lexical level, hard and fast lines between syntax and semantics are artificial at best; and systems which want to reason not only about what they hear and say, but also about how they hear and say it, must know at least as much about words as they must know about their domains.

The work reported here involves developing representation schemes for lexical information, in which all lexical information is represented in a single, unified network, accessible to the same retrieval and inference mechanisms as domain information. The lexicons under discussion are being built using semi-automated techniques from machine readable dictionaries; the representation is intended to support medium scale (semi-realistic) lexicons for a wide range of purposes. (Full, realistic sized lexicons require substantial back-end support because of problems of scale.)

We begin from the linguistic theory of the relational lexicon. Lexical relations provide a formal mechanism for expressing relations among concepts. Traditionally, lexical relations have been approached as a means for representing semantic information about words. Our approach extends the theory of lexical relations to embrace syntactic and morphological as well as semantic relations. In addition, our research has uncovered a rich structure to the realm of lexical relations which has not heretofore been noted or exploited. We begin by describing that theory, and the extensions to it which have resulted from this work. The resulting hierarchy of lexical relations may be thought of as a kind of structural primitives, which represent cognitive relations among lexical items.

Moving from the theory of lexical relations, we describe how information about the lexical relation hierarchy is represented in SNePS network. Next we show how information about specific words is integrated into the hierarchy network, resulting in a large network containing a (potentially dynamic) lexicon, with syntactic, semantic, and morphological information all readily available. The resulting representation distinguishes among homonym labels, words, strings representing word spellings, and word senses, allowing the kinds of reasoning about words that people routinely make. The representation used has several unusual features, among them the clear importance of path-based inference. We discuss trade-offs between heavy concentration of path-based inference (especially in very large lexicons) versus use of some relational axioms and node-based inference. Finally we detail applications for this lexicon in information retrieval, in natural language generation, and in natural language front-ends to database management systems.

2   The Theory of Lexical Relations

Lexical relations form the heart of a formal theory for expressing relations among concepts. Apresyan, Mel'čuk, and Žolkovsky launched a wide study of lexical and semantic relationships in Russian as part of developing the *Explanatory Combinatory Dictionary* (*ECD*) [AMZ69]. Their goal was to develop a theory of word meaning which would suffice for providing definitions for all terms in what they viewed as a wholly new kind of unilingual dictionary. The designers of the *ECD* began from the position that dictionaries ought to support a variety of tasks which traditionally they do not support well, including reflecting all the lexical information needed to form a text. Because they were trying to develop an entirely new kind of dictionary, Mel'čuk's team did not begin, as lexicographers frequently do, by examining other dictionaries. Instead they looked for their relations in the language itself, then tested the completeness of their theory in terms of whether they could in fact develop their dictionary. Their effort thus represents a linguistic investigation into (at least some aspects of) the semantics of word use,and the result is a theory of meaning. Lexical relations also play a key role in Mel'čuk's more recent "meaning ⟺ text" model [Mel73], and Mel'čuk has recently led a similar dictionary effort for Canadian French. Evens and Smith [ES79] describes a wide range of early work in lexical relation theory.

A fundamental concept behind relational lexicons is that as much as possible of the information in the lexicon is represented directly in terms of lexical relations among words or word senses. Classical work in the literature concentrates on semantic relations. The actual significance of this stress originally lay in two areas. The first had to do with the lay-out of *ECD* definitions. As in more familiar dictionaries, the *ECD* separated syntactic and semantic information within definitions. But secondly, and more centrally, the designers wanted a mechanism as formal and structured as those usually applied to syntactic information to represent semantics. When we go outside the task of building the *ECD*, however, the stress on semantic relations no longer appears appropriate. We have said above that the separation between syntax and semantics is as artificial for words as it is for larger texts. A relational lexicon which contains only semantic information would essentially reproduce the current bifurcated arrangement for on-line lexicons, with syntactic and semantic information artificially segregated. Rather than continue in this outdated tradition, we have chosen to view lexical relations more broadly.

Taking this view has led to an analysis of lexical relations which reveals far more structure within the relations themselves than previous researchers have remarked. We have uncovered a rich hierarchy or over a hundred relations, with an overall hierarchy depth of around five, and over twenty substantive categories at the next to leaf level [Nut89a]. We view this snapshot of the hierarchy as essentially incomplete in two different ways. First, the current snapshot is misleadingly neat. Our work leads us to believe that the actual hierarchy is not a tree, as our present report suggests, but a tangled hierarchy, with an even richer internal structure than we have documented. Second, we believe that the class of relations itself is probably open, including many relations we have not identified, some of which are domain-specific, and evolve as their domains do. The hierarchy with which we are working now we view as a core of a potentially richer and dynamic structure. This view influences our representation strongly, in that we want representations which will support both tangled hierarchies and dynamic enrichment. Lexical relations are not just a shorthand for giving information about words. They are also themselves objects of knowledge, which our representation should also directly reflect.

3 Representing the Relational Hierarchy

The relational hierarchy is a fairly straightforward instance of a hierarchical knowledge structure. At the present level of development, the most common hierarchical relationships involved are most obviously viewed as set membership and subset/superset relations. The one trap to avoid lies in representing the hierarchical information in the same way as one would represent, for instance, the information (derived from whatever source, but construed as part of the lexicon) that dogs are mammals. There are two problems here.

One is a relatively simple problem of recursion in representation. Since lexical relations are themselves objects of knowledge, within the SNePS formalism, they should be represented by nodes, not arcs. Now say that we represent the relation between 'Mt. Rushmore' and 'mountain' by something like an *arg1-arg2-rel* frame, with a *rel* arc to a node called something like 'member', which represents the lexical relation which holds between 'Mt. Rushmore' and 'mountain'. Now how do we say that the lexical relation 'member' belongs to the class of taxonomic lexical relations? If we try to use the same 'member' node as the first argument and also as the relation, we wind up with a pathological proposition node.

The reason this is a problem, and not a blunder, is that the lexical relation is not really the same thing that holds between itself and its parent class. The problem here is one of distinguishing metalevel information about the lexical relation hierarchy from object level information which we use it to represent. We can see the importance of distinguishing them if we look at the consequences of trying to use path-based inference to implement inheritance down hierarchical subtrees. When we construct a path-based rule to make all object property markers behave alike in some respect, we don't want to have to filter for instances of membership like 'Mt. Rushmore' to 'mountain', or of subset like 'dog' to 'mammal'.

Figure 1 shows a the SNePS representation for a fragment of the lexical relation hierarchy. Throughout the examples, we adopt several node naming conventions for simplicity. Node names in all capitals represent members of the lexical relations hierarchy. Proposition nodes are numbered beginning with m1 in the traditional way. Other node names in lower case represent word sense nodes.

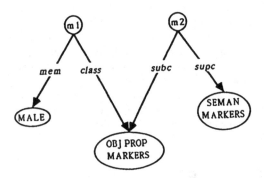

Figure 1: Representation of Hierarchical Facts.

4   Representing Lexical Information

Information about words takes several forms. The first, and simplest, is lexical relation instances. This information encodes everything from taxonomic classification relations (including relations like TAXON, which closely corresponds to the traditional IS-A link, but also synonymy relations, antonymy relations, and others) to generic role relations (for instance the Act/Actor relation, which holds e.g. between "bake" and "baker") to morphological and syntactic relations such as the State/Verb relation which holds between a nominalized verb and its verb. The second kind of information could be viewed as collapsed lexical relations, and covers such relatively simple markers as part of speech (associated with sense nodes), alternate spellings (relation between a headword node and a string node), and the like. The third reflects information about the sense-subsense hierarchy. This is the familiar dictionary definition hierarchy, under which a word may have more specific senses which represent refinements on more general ones.

Representing lexical relation instances within the network is now simply a matter of adding in frames (proposition nodes) asserting the various instances. Lexical relation instances ("A merino is a kind of sheep", or "TAXON(merino, sheep))" are canonically represented using *arg1-arg2-rel* frames for nonsymmetric relations ("lamb is the young of sheep", i.e., YOUNG-OF(lamb, sheep)) or *argument-argument-rel* frames for symmetric ones ("sheepfold and sheepcote are synonyms", i.e., SYN{sheepfold, sheepcote}; note that SYN takes a set, not a tuple). We represent information about the sense-subsense hierarchy using an obvious *sense-subsense* frame; miscellaneous information such as part of speech and alternate spellings currently have specialized frames, but will probably eventually be represented in the same way as lexical relation instances (i.e. treating the information as possibly degenerate – one place – lexical relations).

We now integrate all three kinds of information about words into the hierarchy network in the obvious way. Figure 2 represents a digested form of the information about some words related to the most common sense of "sheep" as derived from definitions in *Webster's Seventh Collegiate Dictionary*. Note that this sense of "sheep" has a subsense, which covers only a single species. We have omitted all nodes and arcs above the sense level (i.e. headword and string nodes and their associated frames) for simplicity, and collapsed parts of the lexical relation hierarchy (especially in nodes m4 and m5) to make the figure more readable.

The resulting lexicon can be used either as stand-alone support for some external activity (such as automated query expansion for information retrieval) or as an integral part of the knowledge base for a natural language system. For the second option, which is the more interesting, the remaining information in the knowledge base is integrated into the lexicon representation, with semantic information relating to senses hanging off the appropriate nodes. The result is a knowledge base which not only has ideas and knows what words are typically used to represent them (the effect of using something like *lex* arcs in a more traditional SNePS-ish representation), but knows about those words and can reason on the basis of its knowledge.

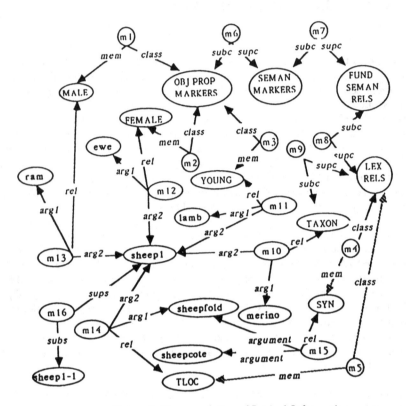

Figure 2: Representation of Lexical Information.

5 Inference in the Lexicon: Path-Based Methods versus Relational Axioms

One of the interesting features of this representation is that it is in some ways more obviously associational than many semantic network representations. That is, in SNePS knowledge bases in general, node based inference tends to dominate, leaving path-based methods as afterthoughts or efficiency hacks. This balance contributes towards the tendency to view semantic networks (of whatever brand) as "notational variants of predicate logic".

When reasoning within and using the lexicon knowledge base, however, path-based reasoning suddenly emerges as the primary natural mode. If, for instance, we are engaged in word choice, it is natural to string through synonym paths; similarly for finding morphological variants – or, for instance, locating a possible synonym for a nominal verb by looking for the nominalized form of a synonym for the base verb. The resulting paths become extremely complex, with many restrictions; but the essential pattern of reasoning is arrow chasing, not unification-based pattern matching. Perhaps this should not be surprising, since Quillian's pioneering work in associational networks was inspired by reflections on connections in word meanings [Qui67]. From that perspective, though, it does seem perverse that the lexicons for semantic network based natural language systems have traditionally been isolated from the networks.

There are natural applications for node-based reasoning within the lexicon, however. In particular, there is interesting information about the lexical relations themselves beyond their positions in the hierarchy. Evens's work [ES79] [AE84] [EVW85] has led to a view in which a great deal of information about the lexical relations is expressed in relational axioms. For instance, a relational axiom for the lexical relation YOUNG-OF might be expressed by saying that for all x and y, if YOUNG-OF(x,y) then for all z, if z is an x, then z is a y and z is young. (An axiom like this would let the lexicon infer, from the fact that O'Grady is a puppy and YOUNG-OF(puppy,dog), that O'Grady is a young dog). Obviously, we would like our system to have at least that much common sense, if it is to behave like a knowledge based lexicon.

Combining node-based and path-based inference mechanisms works well in small versions of this lexicon. At present, an ongoing project is building a master version of the lexicon, using semi-automated techniques and working from machine readable dictionaries [FNA+88] [AE88] [NFE89] [Nut89b]. The resulting network is expected to have on the order of 2^{30} nodes. Working with networks of this size presents obvious difficulties (beginning with overrunning the LISP hash table and the addressable dimensions of unix paging algorithms), many of which can be overcome by customizing the architecture to large size (using our own order-preserving minimal perfect hashing functions to intern nodes instead of relying on the language [FHC89], for instance). But when we have done all we can to improve memory management and large scale efficiency at the implementation level, we are left with the obvious problem that full scale unification on something that size will never perform acceptably, on any implementation, on any hardware. At that point, for applications which want really large lexicons, the prospect of largely replacing node-based by path-based inference methods becomes particularly intriguing.

6   Applications for the Lexicon

The lexicon we are building is intended to support many different applications which involve natural language. The original motivating application behind much of the work on lexical relations in the group at Virginia Tech and related work in Evens's group at Illinois Institute of Technology has been automated query expansion for information retrieval. One of the major problems in information retrieval is poor match between the user's query and document index terms. The problem, essentially, is that information retrieval systems index on words, not ideas. So for instance a user who asked about sheep raising would not get a document that was indexed on merino breeding, unless it also happened to indexed on sheep. The network above, together with some simple path-based rules, could easily be used to expand a query about sheep to recognize that "merino" was a related term (and so should be searched on), as well as picking up "ram", "ewe", "lamb", and, with the obvious extensions, "wool" and "mutton". There is preliminary evidence [Fox80] [EVW85] that expanding queries using lexical relations improves information retrieval. Further studies are investigating what kinds of expansions may prove particularly useful.

In addition to query expansion, of course, a lexicon such as the one reported here could be used to enhance original document indexing. The great stumbling block here is disambiguation. Again, there are preliminary results [CL85] indicating that this problem may be tractable, but it is far from solved, and we are not currently working on it.

Outside information retrieval, however, there are many potential uses for a knowledge based lexicon. A separate project at Virginia Tech, at present in its very early stages, is examining natural language connected text generation. We are currently looking into ways to apply the lexicon to this work as well. In particular, in the long run, we want to be able to reason about the text being produced and the words being used to produce it, as well as the concepts being expressed and their (abstract, high level) expression. We anticipate substantial power from having information about the language explicitly at the system's command. Natural language understanding systems could similarly benefit.

Part of our motivation in this project has been to build a lexicon which will be reusable. To date, most efforts in developing on-line lexicons have been specialized to a single program; the idea of having one lexicon which could support more than one application seems to have received little consideration. Yet when we go beyond toy systems, building lexicons becomes a serious problem in and of itself. It seems desirable, then, the place our effort into building a product which, once made, can be used for any purpose for which we want lexicons at all.

Furthermore, we do not see these applications as ultimately separate. In particular, the CODER project [Fox87] [FF87] intends to combine document analysis and representation, natural language interface with users, automated query expansion, and natural language responses to users, including explanations of the system's actions, into a single distributed AI system. This system needs to do all the tasks listed above: it must index documents, expand queries and retrieve documents, understand (limited) natural language input, and produce (at least some) connected text output. Under the circumstances, the gain from a single lexicon to support all these activities is clear.

7   Conclusions

Linguistic understanding of structures of form and meaning at the word level has tended to lag behind similar studies at the sentence and higher level. This has partly been true because there is a temptation to think that the word level is trivial, or easily managed. Yet when we actually come to grips with it, it tends to pose many of the same problems encountered elsewhere plus many of its own. It is only relatively recently that coherent linguistic theories of the lexicon have begun to emerge.

It should therefore surprise no one that computational approaches to lexicography have been crude compared to the representations used for sentence and higher level syntax and semantics. But we are now reaching the point where we are developing systems sophisticated enough to be frustrated by their crude lexicons. The model of the lexicon which has predominated to date, which consists essentially of a lightly marked word list and a set of largely segregated, thin and unconvincing semantic representations, becomes less and less satisfying.

The current work builds on a new linguistic theory of the structure of meaning, to emerge with more sophisticated and complete representations of information about words. The result is not simply a bigger, more strongly marked word list, but a genuine knowledge base of information about words, their string representations, and their meanings, which can be integrated with other knowledge to allow simultaneous reasoning about the domain and about the language which can be used to describe it. Research is currently underway to show how much use such a lexicon will ultimately prove.

References

[AE84]   T.E. Ahlswede and M.W. Evens. A lexicon for a medical expert system. In M.W. Evens, editor, *Proceedings of the Workshop on Relational Models of the Lexicon*, page (to appear), July 1984.

[AE88]   T.E. Ahlswede and M.W. Evens. Generating a relational lexicon from a machine-readable dictionary. *International Journal of Lexicography*, 1(3):214–237, 1988.

[AMZ69]   Y.D. Apresyan, I.A. Mel'čuk, and A.K. Zolkovsky. Semantics and lexicography: Towards a new type of unilingual dictionary. In F. Kiefer, editor, *Studies in Syntax and Semantics*, pages 1–33. D. Reidel, Dordrecht, Holland, 1969.

[CL85]   Y. Choueka and S. Lusignan. Disambiguation by short contexts. *Computers and the Humanities*, 19(3):147–157, 1985.

[ES79]   M.W. Evens and R.N. Smith. A lexicon for a computer question-answering system. *American Journal of Computational Linguistics*, Microfiche 83:1–93, 1979.

[EVW85]   M.W. Evens, J. Vandendorpe, and Y.-C. Wang. Lexical-semantic relations in information retrieval. In S. Williams, editor, *Humans and Machines: The Interface through Language*, pages 73–100. Ablex, Norwood, NJ, 1985.

[FF87]   E.A. Fox and R.K. France. Architecture of an expert system for composite document analysis, representation, and retrieval. *International Journal of Approximate Reasoning*, 1:151–175, 1987.

[FHC89]   E.A. Fox, L.S. Heath, and Q.F. Chen. An o(n log n) algorithm for finding minimal perfect hash functions. Department of Computer Science Technical Report 89-10, Virginia Polytechnic Institute and State University, Blacksburg, VA 24061-0106, 1989.

[FNA+88] E.A. Fox, J.T. Nutter, T.E. Ahlswede, M.W. Evens, and J.A. Markowitz. Building a large thesaurus for information retrieval. In *Proceedings of the Second Conference on Applied Natural Language Processing*, pages 101–108. Association for Computational Linguistics, February 1988.

[Fox80]   E.A. Fox. Lexical relations: enhancing effectiveness of information retrieval. *ACM SIGIR Forum*, 15(3):6–35, 1980.

[Fox87]   E.A. Fox. Development of the CODER system: A testbed for artificial intelligence methods in information retrieval. *Information Processing and Management*, 23(4):341–366, 1987.

[Mel73]   I.A. Mel'čuk. Towards a linguistic 'meaning text' model. In F. Kiefer, editor, *Trends in Soviet Theoretical Linguistics*, pages 33–57. D. Reidel, 1973.

[NFE89]   J.T. Nutter, E.A. Fox, and M.W. Evens. Building a lexicon from machine-readable dictionaries for improved information retrieval. In *The Dynamic Text: 16th ALLC and 9th ICCH International Conferences*, page (to appear), June 1989.

[Nut89a]   J.T. Nutter. A lexical relation hierarchy. Department of Computer Science Technical Report 89-6, Virginia Polytechnic Institute and State University, Blacksburg, VA 24061-0106, 1989.

[Nut89b]   J.T. Nutter. Representing knowledge about words. In *Proceedings of the Second National Conference of AI and Cognitive Science*, page (to appear), September 1989.

[Qui67]   M.R. Quillian. Word concepts: A theory and simulation of some basic semantic capabilities. *Behavioral Science*, 12:410–430, 1967.

REPRESENTING FICTION IN SNePS

William J. Rapaport
Department of Computer Science
and Center for Cognitive Science
State University of New York at Buffalo
Buffalo, NY 14260
rapaport@cs.buffalo.edu

Abstract

This paper discusses issues in the representation of fictional entities and the representation of propositions from fiction, using SNePS. It briefly surveys four philosophical ontological theories of fiction and sketches an epistemological theory of fiction (to be implemented in SNePS) using a story operator and rules for allowing propositions to "migrate" into and out of story "spaces".

1 A Computational Approach to Fiction

This paper will discuss issues in the representation of fictional entities and the representation of propositions from fiction, using SNePS.

As part of the SUNY Buffalo Graduate Group in Cognitive Science's project on Cognitive and Computer Systems for Understanding Narrative Text, we are constructing a computational cognitive agent, Cassie, implemented in SNePS (Shapiro 1979, Shapiro & Rapaport 1987 and forthcoming), who will be able to read a narrative and comprehend the indexical information in it, specifically, *where* the events in the narrative are taking place (in the world of the narrative), *when* they take place (in the time-line of the narrative), *who* the participants in these events are (the characters in the world of the narrative), and *from whose point of view* the events and characters are described (Bruder et al. 1986, Rapaport et al. 1989ab).

In order to do this, Cassie has to be able to (1) read a narrative (in particular, a fictional narrative), (2) build a mental-model representation of the story and the story-world, and (3) use that mental model to understand and to answer questions about the narrative. To build the mental model, she will need to contribute something to her understanding of the story. One contribution is in the form of a "deictic center"—a data structure that contains the indexical information needed to track the who, when, and where.

Another contribution—one of the foci of this paper—is background knowledge about the real world. For instance, if Cassie is reading a novel about the Civil War, she would presumably bring to her understanding of it some knowledge of the Civil War, such as that Abraham Lincoln was the 16th president and was assassinated in 1865, even if that information is not explicitly stated in the novel. The novel might go on to make other claims about Lincoln, such as that he had a particular conversation with General Grant on a particular day in 1860 (even if, in fact, they never talked on that day—this is a novel, after all). Such a claim would probably not be inconsistent with anything Cassie antecedently believed about Lincoln. But some claims in the novel might be thus inconsistent, e.g., if she read that Lincoln was re-elected to a third term in 1868. So Cassie has to be able to represent the information presented in the narrative, keep it suitably segregated from her background knowledge, yet be able to have information from her antecedent beliefs "migrate" into her model of the story world as well as have information from the story world "migrate" back into her store of beliefs about the real world.

There have been a number of theories in philosophy about the nature of fictional objects. All of these are *ontological* theories concerned with such questions as: What are fictional objects? How can they have properties? How are they related to non-fictional entities? However, for the purposes of our project, we need to be more concerned with "epistemological" or processing/computational/interpretive issues: How does a reader understand a (fictional) narrative? How does a reader decide whether and to what extent it *is* fictional? How does a reader construct a mental model of the story world? How does a reader represent fictional entities and their properties? How does a reader integrate his or her knowledge of the real world with what s/he reads in the narrative? And so on. Some of these are, indeed, ontological issues, but they are what I have elsewhere termed issues in "epistemological ontology" (Rapaport 1985/1986): Corresponding to the purely or *metaphysically* ontological question, "What *are* fictional objects?", we ask the *epistemologically* ontological question, "How does a cognitive agent *represent* fictional objects?". And corresponding to the purely ontological question, "How are properties *predicated* of fictional objects?", we ask the epistemologically ontological question, "How does a cognitive agent *represent* the properties of fictional objects?"

In this paper, I examine several philosophical theories of fiction to see what aspects of them are useful for our cognitive/computational project, and I will propose a representation scheme, in SNePS, that satisfactorily answers most of the kinds of questions raised above (and that incorporates an exciting, if counterintuitive, proposal for the remaining questions!). Specifically, the proposal is to embed the propositions of the fictional narrative in a "story operator" that is formally akin to the belief representations we already have in SNePS. I will show how SNePS's propositional and fully intensional nature, plus the story operator, allow the best aspects of the philosophical theories to be implemented.

2 Four Ontological Theories of Fiction

Let me begin by briefly surveying four (out of many, many more) philosophical theories of the ontological status of fictional objects. I will not be concerned so much with criticizing them (though I will mention some difficulties they have), as I will with finding what aspects of them might be useful for our, rather different, purposes.

2.1 Castañeda's Theory

Hector-Neri Castañeda's theory of guises and consubstantiation is an all-encompassing theory of the objects of thought as well as of the objects in the world (Castañeda 1972, 1975ab, 1977, 1980,

1989), which includes a theory of fictional objects (Castañeda 1979, 1989). I have discussed this theory in more detail elsewhere (Rapaport 1978, 1985b), so I will content myself with a presentation of his theory of fiction here.

Castañeda takes a uniform viewpoint, with which I agree: All objects in fiction are to be treated alike, whether they are "real" or "fictional" (cf. Scholes 1968, Rapaport 1985a); they are, in his terminology, "guises", i.e., roughly, intensional objects of thought. But there are different modes of predication of properties to guises. Thus, if I read in a narrative about the Civil War that Lincoln died in 1865, this would be analyzed in his theory as a "consubstantiation" (C*) of two guises, the guise c{being Lincoln} (i.e., the intensional object of thought whose sole internal property is *being Lincoln*) and the guise c{being Lincoln, having died in 1865} (i.e., the intensional object of thought whose sole internal properties are *being Lincoln* and *having died in 1865*):

$$C^*(c\{\text{being Lincoln}\}, c\{\text{being Lincoln, having died in 1865}\})$$

Consubstantiation is an existence-entailing equivalence relation. On the other hand, if I read another narrative in which the author has stated that Lincoln was re-elected in 1868, this would be analyzed as a "consociation" (C**) of two guises:

$$C^{**}(c\{\text{being Lincoln}\}, c\{\text{being Lincoln, having being re-elected in 1868}\})$$

Consociation is a non–existence-entailing equivalence relation among guises that are "joined together" in a mind. But it is the *same* Lincoln (i.e., c{being Lincoln}) in both cases.

That is a rather drastic oversimplification, but it raises the following concern: How is the reader to decide whether a sentence read in the course of a narrative is to be analyzed by consubstantiation or by consociation? In fact, the uniformity with respect to the *objects* should be extended to the mode of predication: All predications in narrative are consociation-like, even the "true" ones.

Castañeda also admits the existence of "story operators" into his theory, but finds them otiose. A story operator is a (usually modal) operator that prefixes all sentences in a narrative: 'In story S, it is the case that φ'. Not all theorists of fiction find them attractive (cf. Rapaport 1976, 1985a), but, as Castañeda points out, one can hardly deny that they exist: Take as 'S' the title page of the narrative! His claim is that they fail to account for the interesting or problematic aspects of fiction.

An example in the context of SNePS might clarify things a bit. Consider the situation illustrated in Example 1. Suppose that Cassie has a background belief ("world knowledge", as we might say) that

(1) George Washington was the first president.

This would be analyzed as a consubstantiation. Suppose next that Cassie reads in a narrative that

(2) George Washington chopped down a cherry tree.

This would be analyzed as a consociation. The *processing* problem is that, if both sentences were to have occurred in the narrative, they would have to be treated *alike*, using the *same* mode of predication, namely, consociation. But there are no other problems, and, so far, all is well.

2.2   Lewis's Theory

David Lewis's theory of fiction (Lewis 1978) makes essential use of the story operator, and, despite my misgivings about them in an earlier life (see the references above), I now find that they have a useful role to play. But Lewis's version has some problems. He allows his story operator to be dropped *by way of abbreviation*. Thus, we might say

> Sherlock Holmes lived at 221B Baker Street,

but what we really mean is, say,

> In *The Hound of the Baskervilles*, Sherlock Holmes lived at 221B Baker Street,

since, after all, the former is false and the latter is true.

There is an evident advantage to this, for it enables us to distinguish between "facts" about fictional and non-fictional entities, a worthy endeavor, and one that Cassie must be able to do. In fact, she will do it much the way that Lewis recommends. Consider the following argument:

> Lived-at(221B Baker St., Sherlock Holmes)
> 221B Baker St. = a bank
> ∴ Lived-at(a bank, Sherlock Holmes)

This is clearly invalid, although the first premise is true (by story-operator elimination) and the second may be presumed to be true for the sake of the argument. *Merely* replacing the story operator won't help:

> In *The Hound of the Baskervilles*, Lived-at(221B Baker St., Sherlock Holmes)
> 221B Baker St. = a bank
> ∴ In *The Hound of the Baskervilles*, Lived-at(a bank, Sherlock Holmes)

fares no better. Nor does:

> In *The Hound of the Baskervilles*, Lived-at(221B Baker St., Sherlock Holmes)
> 221B Baker St. = a bank
> ∴ Lived-at(a bank, Sherlock Holmes)

But a *uniform* treatment of the story operator works fine:

> In *The Hound of the Baskervilles*, Lived-at(221B Baker St., Sherlock Holmes)
> In *The Hound of the Baskervilles*, 221B Baker St. = a bank
> ∴ In *The Hound of the Baskervilles*, Lived-at(a bank, Sherlock Holmes)

and

> Lived-at(221B Baker St., Sherlock Holmes)
> 221B Baker St. = a bank
> ∴ Lived-at(a bank, Sherlock Holmes)

are both valid, albeit unsound.

The difficulty with Lewis's proposal is that

Sherlock Holmes is fictional

is false no matter how you slice it. It's false *with* the story operator restored, since, *within the story*, Holmes is as real as anyone is. And it's false (or at least truth-valueless) *without* it, since 'Sherlock Holmes' is a non-denoting expression. This difficulty is unacceptable.

2.3 Parsons's Theory

Terence Parsons's theory of fiction (Parsons 1975, 1980) is based on his theory of nonexistent objects. In contrast to Castañeda, who has one kind of property but two modes of predication, Parsons has two kinds of properties (nuclear and extranuclear) but only one mode of predication. Rather than rehearse his full theory of fiction here (see Rapaport 1985a, for a summary and critique), I shall focus on a distinction he makes between "native", "immigrant", and "surrogate" fictional objects.

Native fictional objects are, roughly, those who originate in the story in which they are found, such as Sherlock Holmes in *The Hound of the Baskervilles*. Immigrant fictional objects are, roughly, those who have migrated into a story from elsewhere, such as London in *The Hound of the Baskervilles* or Sherlock Holmes in *The Seven Per Cent Solution*. But, of course, the London of *The Hound of the Baskervilles* has properties that the real London lacks (and vice versa), which raises obvious difficulties; so the London-of-*The-Hound-of-the-Baskervilles* is a surrogate fictional object, distinct from the real London.

Such distinctions can be made and are no doubt useful. But there are a number of questions that have to be answered before one can accept them: Which London did Conan Doyle discuss? Which London did Sherlock Holmes and Dr. Watson discuss? When is one discussing London and when the London-of-*The-Hound-of-the-Baskervilles*? In general, how does the reader distinguish properties of the "real" London from the properties of the London-of-*The-Hound-of-the-Baskervilles*? These are questions that can be dealt with, I believe, in the SNePS proposal to be introduced below.

2.4 Van Inwagen's Theory

The final theory of fictional objects in our brief survey is one that I find quite congenial in many respects, though it, too, falls short. Peter van Inwagen's theory (van Inwagen 1977), like Castañeda's, distinguishes between two modes of predication, and, like Lewis's, it uses something like a story operator.

The two modes of predication are "predication" and "ascription". 'Sherlock Holmes is fictional' expresses a property *predicated of* an existing theoretical entity of literary criticism, namely, Sherlock Holmes. (Other kinds of theoretical entities of literary criticism include novels, short stories, etc.) In contrast, 'Sherlock Holmes is a detective' expresses (perhaps elliptically) a property *ascribed to* the same theoretical entity of literary criticism *in* a work of fiction:

A(detective, Sherlock Holmes, *The Hound of the Baskervilles*)

Note that the story is not strictly speaking a logical operator, but an essential argument place in a 3-place predication relation.

There are two problems with this otherwise quite nice theory. They are, I believe, not serious problems and could be easily gotten around. First, suppose that Hintikka, say, writes an essay (call it "Was Holmes a Good Logician?") on the Sherlock Holmes stories in which he concludes that, despite what is popularly taken to be the case, Sherlock Holmes is illogical. According to van Inwagen's theory, contrary to what one might expect, it is *not* the case that

A(illogical, Sherlock Holmes, "Was Holmes a Good Logician?").

Why? Because "Was Holmes a Good Logician?" is not literature. This strikes me as an unnecessary aspect of van Inwagen's theory.

Second, assume that in *War and Peace* it is stated that Napolean is vain. (It may be so stated; I confess to not (yet) having read it. It might suffice for van Inwagen's example that it follow (logically) from what is stated in *War and Peace* that Napolean is vain; no matter.) But, according to van Inwagen's theory and again contrary to what one might expect, it is *not* the case that

A(vain, Napolean, *War and Peace*),

because Napolean is not a theoretical entity of literary criticism! Again, this strikes me as unnecessary.

3   A SNePS Approach to Fiction

In order for Cassie to read a narrative, the knowledge representations she should construct will include a story operator (like Lewis or van Inwagen), only one mode of predication (like Parsons), and only one kind of property (like Castañeda). Since, at the time of writing, this theory is only beginning to be implemented, there is a strong possibility that this will prove insufficient: The one addition that I can foresee (urged by me in earlier writings, e.g., Rapaport 1976, 1985a, and suggested to me by Johan Lammens) is the need to distinguish between real-world entities and their surrogates; but it must be kept in mind that all entities represented in Cassie's mind are just that—entities in her mind—*not* entities some of which are real and some of which are fictional.

The story operator will set up a "story space" that is formally equivalent to a belief space (cf. Rapaport 1986, Wiebe & Rapaport 1986, Shapiro & Rapaport forthcoming). It will allow Cassie to distinguish her own beliefs about London from (her beliefs about) claims made about London in a story in precisely the same way that belief spaces allow Cassie to distinguish her own beliefs about Lucy from her beliefs about John's beliefs about Lucy (cf. Rapaport 1986, Shapiro & Rapaport 1987).

But how should this be handled? Consider Example 2a. Suppose that one of Cassie's background beliefs is that Lincoln died in 1865 and that she reads in a narrative that Lincoln was re-elected in 1868. There is a processing problem: Cassie is faced with an inconsistency. There are two solutions. First, the SNePS Belief Revision system (SNeBR; Martins & Shapiro 1988) can be invoked. The detection of the inconsistency will cause a split to be made into two (consistent) contexts. But note that the net effect of this is to embed the second statement (the re-election in 1868) in a story operator. So why not start with a story operator in the first place? This is the second solution, as shown in Example 2b.

But now let's complicate the data a bit. Consider Example 3. Suppose that Cassie's background beliefs include both that Lincoln was the 16th president and that Lincoln died in 1865, and suppose once again that Cassie reads in a narrative that Lincoln was re-elected in 1868. The processing "problem" here (it is not really a problem) is that we want the first of Cassie's two background beliefs to "migrate into" the story world. The reason that this is not a problem is that those first two background beliefs are *Cassie's* beliefs and the third is not. The first one (that Lincoln was 16th president) is both believed by Cassie *and* is in the story world.

Consider Example 1 again. If Cassie knows that she is reading a narrative, we want it to be the case that she believes (1) (that Washington was the first president), and we want both (1) and (2) (that he chopped down the cherry tree) to be in the story world. How do we accomplish this? By *starting* with a story operator on (2). In general, *we will put a story operator on* all *narrative predications*.

But then we face two problems: Background beliefs of the reader are normally brought to bear on understanding the story, as we saw in Example 2 (cf. Rapaport et al. 1989a). And we often come to learn (or, at least, come to have beliefs) about the real world from reading fictional narratives. Thus, we need to have two rules, which I will put roughly, but boldly, as follows:

(R1) Propositions *outside* the story space established by the story operator (i.e., antecedently believed by the reader) are assumed, *when necessary*, to hold *within* that story space *by default* and *defeasibly*.

(R2) Propositions *inside* the story space are assumed, *when necessary*, to hold *outside* the that story space *by default* and *defeasibly*.

Some comments: The "when necessary" clause (suggested by Stuart C. Shapiro) is there to prevent an explosion in the size of belief and story spaces; the migrations permitted by these two rules would only take place on an as-needed basis for understanding the story or for understanding the world around us. The "by default" clause is there for obvious reasons: we wouldn't want to have Lincoln's dying in 1865 migrate into a narrative in which he is re-elected in 1868. The "defeasibly" clause is there to undo any damage that might be done at a later point in the narrative if such a migration had taken place, innocently, at an earlier point. Rule (R1) (or such refinements of it as will, no doubt, be necessary as implementation of the theory proceeds) aids in our understanding of the story. Rule (R2) (or such refinements of it as will, no doubt, be necessary as implementation of the theory proceeds) allows us to enlarge our views of the world from reading literature, while also allowing us to segregate our real-world beliefs from our story-world beliefs.

I will close with a couple of final remarks. First, to see how the story operator solves the problem with Lewis's theory (how it solves the problems with van Inwagen's are left as exercises for the reader), look at Example 4.

Second, in the Examples, I have used the linguist's triangle to hide irrelevant details, but it is worth showing how the story operator looks in detail. This is shown in Figure A.

4 Acknowledgement

This work was supported in part by the National Science Foundation under Grant IRI-8610517. I am grateful to the members of SNeRG and the Graduate Group in Cognitive Science for their contributions and comments. A version of this paper was presented at the 1989 Conference on Problems and Changes in the Concept of Predication (University of California Humanities Research Institute, University of California at Irvine).

5 References

1. Bruder, Gail A.; Duchan, Judith F.; Rapaport, William J.; Segal, Erwin M.; Shapiro, Stuart C.; & Zubin, David A. (1986), "Deictic Centers in Narrative: An Interdisciplinary Cognitive-Science Project," *Technical Report 86-20* (Buffalo: SUNY Buffalo Dept. of Computer Science, September 1986).

2. Castañeda, Hector-Neri (1972), "Thinking and the Structure of the World," *Philosophia* 4 (1974) 3-40; reprinted in 1975 in *Critica* 6 (1972) 43-86.

3. Castañeda, Hector-Neri (1975a), "Identity and Sameness," *Philosophia* 5: 121-150.

4. Castañeda, Hector-Neri (1975b), *Thinking and Doing: The Philosophical Foundations of Institutions* (Dordrecht: D. Reidel).

5. Castañeda, Hector-Neri (1977), "Perception, Belief, and the Structure of Physical Objects and Consciousness," *Synthèse* 35: 285-351.

6. Castañeda, Hector-Neri (1979), "Fiction and Reality: Their Fundamental Connections; An Essay on the Ontology of Total Experience," *Poetics* 8: 31-62.

7. Castañeda, Hector-Neri (1980), "Reference, Reality, and Perceptual Fields," *Proceedings and Addresses of the American Philosophical Association* 53: 763-823.

8. Castañeda, Hector-Neri (1989), *Thinking, Language, and Experience* (Minneapolis: University of Minnesota Press).

9. Lewis, David (1978), "Truth in Fiction," *American Philosophical Quarterly* 15: 37-46.

10. Martins, João, & Shapiro, Stuart C. (1988), "A Model for Belief Revision," *Artificial Intelligence* 35: 25-79.

11. Parsons, Terence (1975), "A Meinongian Analysis of Fictional Objects," *Grazer Philosophische Studien* 1: 73-86.

12. Parsons, Terence (1980), *Nonexistent Objects* (New Haven: Yale University Press).

13. Rapaport, William J. (1976), *Intentionality and the Structure of Existence*, Ph.D. dissertation (Bloomington: Indiana Unversity Dept. of Philosophy).

14. Rapaport, William J. (1978), "Meinongian Theories and a Russellian Paradox," *Noûs* 12: 153-180; errata, *Noûs* 13 (1979) 125.

15. Rapaport, William J. (1985a), "To Be and Not To Be," *Noûs* 19: 255-271.

16. Rapaport, William J. (1985b), "Meinongian Semantics for Propositional Semantic Networks," *Proceedings of the 23rd Annual Meeting of the Association for Computational Linguistics* (*University of Chicago*) (Morristown, NJ: Association for Computational Linguistics): 43-48.

17. Rapaport, William J. (1985/1986), "Non-Existent Objects and Epistemological Ontology," *Grazer Philosophische Studien* 25/26: 61-95.

18. Rapaport, William J. (1986), "Logical Foundations for Belief Representation," *Cognitive Science* 10: 371-422.

19. Rapaport, William J.; Segal, Erwin M.; Shapiro, Stuart C.; Zubin, David A.; Bruder, Gail A.; Duchan, Judith F.; Almeida, Michael J.; Daniels, Joyce H.; Galbraith, Mary M.; Wiebe, Janyce M.; & Yuhan, Albert Hanyong (1989a), "Deictic Centers and the Cognitive Structure of Narrative Comprehension," *Technical Report 89-01* (Buffalo: SUNY Buffalo Dept. of Computer Science, March 1989).

20. Rapaport, William J.; Segal, Erwin M.; Shapiro, Stuart C.; Zubin, David A.; Bruder, Gail A.; Duchan, Judith F.; & Mark, David M. (1989b), "Cognitive and Computer Systems for Understanding Narrative Text," *Technical Report 89-07* (Buffalo: SUNY Buffalo Dept. of Computer Science, August 1989).

21. Scholes, Robert (1968), *Elements of Fiction* (New York: Oxford University Press).

22. Shapiro, Stuart C. (1979), "The SNePS Semantic Network Processing System," in N. V. Findler (ed.), *Associative Networks: The Representation and Use of Knowledge by Computers* (New York: Academic Press): 179-203.

23. Shapiro, Stuart C., & Rapaport, William J. (1987), "SNePS Considered as a Fully Intensional Propositional Semantic Network," in N. Cercone & G. McCalla (eds.), *The Knowledge Frontier: Essays in the Representation of Knowledge* (New York: Springer-Verlag): 262-315; earlier version preprinted as *Technical Report No. 85-15* (Buffalo: SUNY Buffalo Department of Computer Science, 1985); shorter version appeared in *Proceedings of the Fifth National Conference on Artificial Intelligence* (*AAAI-86, Philadelphia*) (Los Altos, CA: Morgan Kaufmann): 278-283.

24. Shapiro, Stuart C., & Rapaport, William J. (forthcoming), "Models and Minds: Knowledge Representation for Natural-Language Competence," in R. Cummins & J. Pollock (eds.), *Philosophical AI: Computational Approaches to Reasoning.*

25. van Inwagen, Peter (1977), "Creatures of Fiction," *American Philosophical Quarterly* 14: 299-308.

26. Wiebe, Janyce M., & Rapaport, William J. (1986), "Representing *De Re* and *De Dicto* Belief Reports in Discourse and Narrative," *Proceedings of the IEEE* 74: 1405-1413.

EXAMPLE 1

<u>Background belief:</u>
(1) GW was the first president   (C*)
<u>Narrative claim:</u>
(2) GW chopped down a cherry tree   (C**)

<u>Processing problem:</u>
In narrative, both have to be treated alike;
          <u>same</u> mode of predication (C**)

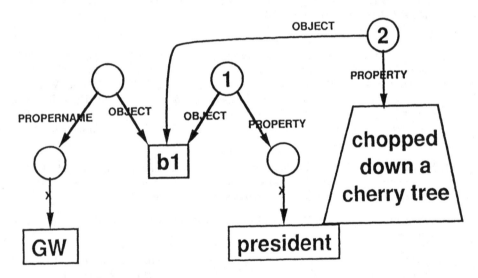

EXAMPLE 2a

Background belief:
(1) Lincoln died in 1865.
Narrative claim:
(2) Lincoln was re-elected in 1868.

Processing problem: inconsistency

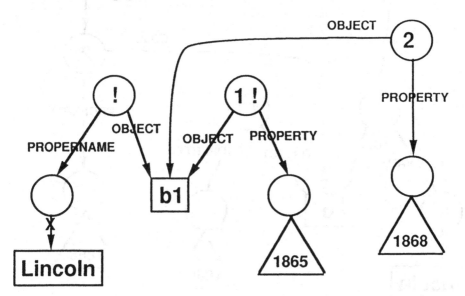

(a) Invoke SNeBR: split into 2 contexts
   Net effect: embed (2) in story-operator

(b) Start with story-operator

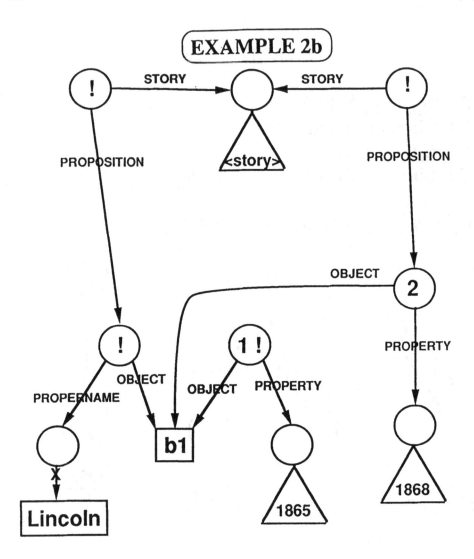

EXAMPLE 3

Background beliefs:
(1) Lincoln was the 16th president.
(2) Lincoln died in 1865.
Narrative claim:
(3) Lincoln was re-elected in 1868.

Processing problem?:
Want (1) to "carry over" to story world.

No problem!: (1), (2) are believed by Cassie;
(1) is believed by her <u>&</u> in story world

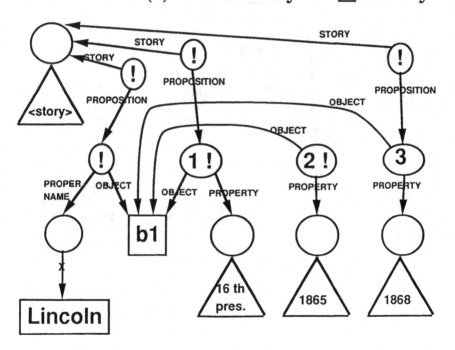

EXAMPLE 4

1. Sherlock Holmes is fictional
2. Sherlock Holmes is a detective.

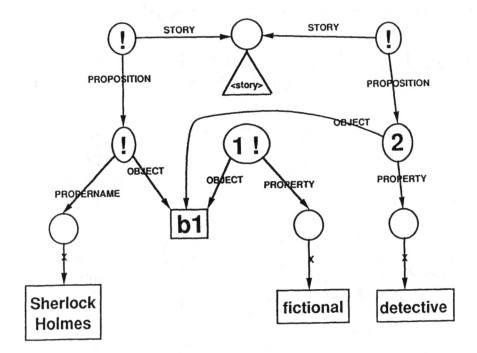

FIGURE A

THE STORY OPERATOR: Details

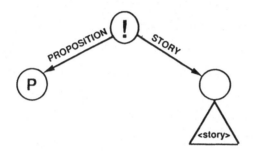

In <story>, P

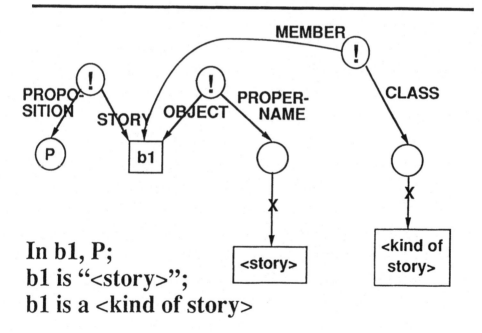

In b1, P;
b1 is "<story>";
b1 is a <kind of story>

Kinds of Opacity and Their Representations*

Richard W. Wyatt

Department of Mathematical and Computer Sciences
West Chester University, PA 19383

Abstract

Examinations of referential opacity have almost invariably focused on propositional attitudes, and even more specifically, on belief sentences. This focus has obscured the fact that there are a number of other kinds of sentences in which the logic-linguistic phenomenon of referential opacity occurs. This paper distinguishes two main kinds of referential opacity and offers distinct representations of their logical forms.

1 Referential Opacity

The *context* in which an occurrence of a referring expression (name, description, etc.,) r in a sentence S occurs is *extensional* if the occurrence of r passes both of the following two tests (cf. Chisholm [2]).

1.1 The Substitutivity of Co-Extensives

An occurrence of r in S passes the test of the Substitutivity of Co-Extensives if and only if the result of replacing the occurrence r by any referring expression that refers (extensionally) to the same thing as r does not change the truth value of S.

For example, consider

    (1)   The Morning Star is blue.

Given that

    (2)   The Morning Star is the Evening Star,

the expression *the Morning Star* can replace *the Evening Star* in (3) to yield

    (3)   The Evening Star is blue.

---

*I want to thank William J. Rapaport and Stuart C. Shapiro for their comments on earlier versions of this work.

Since (3) must have the same truth value as (1), the occurrence of *the Morning Star* in (1) passes the test. On the other hand, the occurrence of *the Morning Star* in

(4)   John believes that the Morning Star is blue,

does not, since

(5)   John believes that the Evening Star is blue,

need not have the same truth value as (4).

1.2   Existential Generalization

The occurrence of the referring expression r in the sentence S passes the test of Existential Generalization if and only if the result of existentially generalizing over the position occupied by r in S follows from S.

For example, the occurrence of *Mary* in

(6)   John knows Mary,

passes the test, because

(7)   There is someone, x, such that John knows x,

follows from (6). On the other hand, the occurrence of *Santa* in

(8)   John seeks Santa,

fails the test, because

(9)   There is someone, x, such that John seeks x,

does *not* follow from (8).

An *intensional context* is one that is *not* extensional. An intensional context is often also called an *opaque* context, and an extensional context, a *transparent* context. In the examples, *the Morning Star* in (1) and *Mary* in (6) occur in extensional or transparent contexts, whereas *the Morning Star* in (4) and *Santa* in (8) occur in intensional or opaque contexts.

2   Examples of Opaque Contexts

In addition to the propositional attitudes, which express an agent's attitude towards some proposition or another, such as

(10)   John believes that the Morning Star is blue,

there is a number of other kinds of referentially opaque sentences; some are given below.

There are intensional, transitive verbs, which express an agent's mental state as regards some object or another, such as

(11)   John loves Mary.

Though John may love Mary, he may hate Lucy, even though unbeknown to him they are one and the same. There are logical modalities, such as

(12)   Necessarily, nine is greater than seven.

Though

(13)   The number of the planets is (identical with) nine,

it does not follow that

(14)   Necessarily, the number of the planets is greater than seven.

And, though they are not generally so regarded, there are the attributive adverbs, those like *quickly* in

(15)   John swam the river quickly.

This treatment of attributive adverbs as generating opacity is new. As will be seen, it rests on the general theory of action proposed by the philosopher Donald Davidson [6], though he himself holds that such adverbs must be excluded from his theory.

According to Davidson, a verb of action refers to an event, an act. In (15) then, John performed a certain act, a swimming of the river. As far as *swimmings* of the river go, his swimming of it was quick. If the time it took John to swim the river is compared to the times it has taken others to *swim* the river, John's time was among the fastest. John's act of swimming the river may, however, also be described as a *crossing* of the river. Thus, we may add the identity statement

(16)   John's swimming of the river is a crossing of the river.

But though his swimming is a crossing, it does not follow that

(17)   John crossed the river quickly.

On the contrary, it is very likely that he *crossed* the river slowly. If the time it took John to cross the river is compared to the times it has taken others to cross the river, which will perhaps include such modes of crossing as rowing, swinging (on a rope), and driving (on a bridge), John's time would no doubt be among the *slowest*.

Finally, some sentences are simply best interpreted as intensional; I term them *intensional sentences*. Consider the sentences

(18)   The Morning Star is blue.

(19)   The Evening Star is red.

(20)   The Morning Star is the Evening Star.

Both (18) and (19) are usually understood in just one way. They are, however, ambiguous. The two interpretations can be illustrated by supposing that

(21)   Nothing is both red and blue.

On the *extensional* interpretation, it follows from (18) – (20) that

(22)   The Morning Star is red.

On the extensional interpretation, (18) – (21) are therefore inconsistent; the one thing is said to be blue *and* red. On the *intensional* interpretation, however, there is no contradiction at all. In this case, *the Morning Star* and *the Evening Star* refer to *intensional* objects, and the properties of one do no longer flow to the other. The intensional interpretation may perhaps be clearer in the case of

(23)   The Morning Star is seen in the morning.

(24)   The Evening Star is not seen in the morning.

These sentences are not inconsistent if *the Morning Star* and *the Evening Star* are understood as referring to *intensional* objects.

There are alternatives to handling the intensional interpretation in terms of intensional objects. Instead of saying that there are two intensional objects, one of which has the property of *being blue* and the other the property of *being red*, one might say that there is just one *extensional* object, which has the two complex properties of *seeming blue if viewed in the morning* and of *seeming red if viewed in the evening*. In a system such as SNePS in which intensional objects are already accepted, however, there is little advantage, and no point, in trying to do without them.

3   Two Kinds of Opacity

I distinguish two different general kinds of referential opacity. The two groups are distinguished according to whether or not sentences are understood as referring to intensional entities. An extensional object is merely one which CASSIE — that is, the SNePS system — holds to be governed by an extensional logic, and an intensional object is one which she holds to be governed by an intensional logic[1].

Another way of distinguishing the two groups is in terms of whether the inference failures associated with the opacity are permanent and unchanging, or whether they are just a matter of some agent's ignorance. For example, consider

(25)   John believes that the Morning Star is blue.

(26)   The Morning Star is the Evening Star.

---

[1]In SNePS, most base nodes can thus be treated as representing *extensional* objects. This view is not the standard SNePS one.

(27)   John believes that the Evening Star is blue.

Certainly, (27) does not follow from (25) and (26). But if John were not ignorant of (26), the inference would go through[2]. On the other hand, consider

(28)   John swam the river quickly.

(29)   John's swimming of the river is (the same act as) his crossing of the river.

(30)   John crossed the river quickly.

Again, (30) does not follow from (28) and (29). But this time, there is nothing which any agent, John or CASSIE or anyone, is ignorant of, but which, were he to know it, the inference would go through. In the first case the inference succeeds or fails depending on whether certain additional information is represented in the network, and so needs to be switched on or off accordingly. In the second case, however, the inference permanently fails. This important difference is sufficient to warrant separate logical forms.

The propositional attitudes and the intensional transitive verbs fall into the first kind, whereas the attributive adverbs and the intensional sentences fall into the second. The logical modalities are a mixed bag. Work is currently in progress towards the development of a theory of naive logical modalities. Such a theory aims to capture the naive and crude grasp that speakers possess of modal notions without the full force of an apparatus as powerful as possible world semantics. The attribution of rich semantic notions such as possible worlds to speakers is questionable, so there is good reason to do without them.

My aim is to provide representations of the *logical form* (cf. Davidson [6], Woods [15] and Moore [10]), of each of these two quite different kinds of referential opacity. It is *not* my aim to provide a complete or detailed *semantic analysis* of the various notions we will be dealing with. I do not, for example, aim to provide a semantic analysis of the propositional attitude *know* in terms of belief and so on (cf. Rapaport, Shapiro and Wiebe [12]) or of the adverb *quickly* in terms of comparisons between the times elapsed for those things said to be quick and those that are not (cf. Cresswell [5]). Though ultimately such details need to be represented, my aim is the more modest one of representing their logical form, the notion of which is now explicated.

To *analyse* an expression is to explain it in terms of, or reduce it to, other concepts of which one presumably has a better grasp. To give the *logical form* of an expression is to depict its inner logical structure, if, indeed, there is any. In giving the logical form, we want to capture enough of the structure to exhibit certain entailments. Here is an example to illustrate the difference.

(31)   A is greater than B.

(32)   B is less than A.

Obviously, (31) and (32) entail one another. In view of

---

[2]Or rather, if we attribute to John the normal inference abilities then we want him to be able to draw the inference.

(33)   For any numbers X and Y, X is greater than Y if and only if Y is
        less than X,

a theory might eliminate one relation in favour of the other. It might therefore represent *less than* in terms of *greater than* (or visa versa).

But though the meanings of these relations are connected by (33), the *structure* of neither is included in that of the other. (32) does not really mean (31); nor does (31) really mean (32). There is, after all, no way to decide which of the two predicates is the *real* primitive and which is the parasite. But more importantly, the representation of (32) via (31) would obscure the crucial difference between[3]

(34)   John believes that if A is greater than B then B is less than A.

(35)   John believes that if A is greater than B then A is greater than B.

A better strategy is therefore to represent both *greater than* and *less than* as simple, irreducible, primitive relations, and to provide, separately and independently, a representation of how they are related; viz., of (33). The relations are thus represented as having the same logical form. Though (31) and (32) entail one another, they do so in virtue of (33) and *not in virtue of their logical form.*

4 Opacity of the First Kind

The two examples of this find of opacity to be considered are the propositional attitudes and the intensional, transitive verbs.

4.1 Rapaport's Representation of Beliefs

In contrast to Wyatt [16], I follow Rapaport [11] and understand the distinction between *de re* beliefs and *de dicto* beliefs in terms of to whom a belief sentence attributes a knowledge of the individuating terms it contains. Thus, in the *de re* sense,

(36)   John believes that the Morning Star is blue,

is understood so that John believes that something which *CASSIE* believes is named *the Morning Star* is blue, whereas in the *de dicto* sense, it is understood so that John believes that something which *John* believes is named *the Morning Star* is blue. In terms of the canonical forms offered by Rapaport [11], the *de re* sense of (36) is expressed by

(37)   Of the Morning Star, John believes that it is blue,

whereas the *de dicto* sense is expressed by

(38)   John believes that Morning Star is blue.

---

[3]This is a form of the *Imputation Problem* discussed by Barnden [1]. A similar difference is noticed by Frege [7].

But though I agree with the way Rapaport draws the distinction between *de re* and *de dicto*, I do not agree with his representations. His representation of

(39)   The Morning Star is blue,

and the *de re* sense of (36) (i.e., of (37)) is given in Figure 1. His representation of (39) and the *de dicto* of (36) (i.e., of (38)) is given in Figure 2.   In addition to some difficulties mentioned

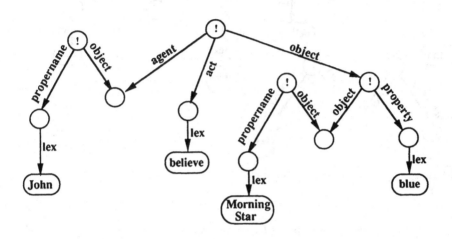

Figure 1: Rapaport's Representations of (37) and (39).

in Wyatt [16], there are the following two, somewhat interconnected, difficulties with Rapaport's representation of beliefs.

4.1.1   First Difficulty

According to Rapaport's theory, the Morning Star in (38) is different from the Morning Star in (39). The idea is that in the *de dicto* sense, (38) is about some entity that the *agent* (John) conceives of, and so requires a new base node to it distinguish it from CASSIE 's concept of the Morning Star[4], referred to in (39). I have previously suggested (Wyatt [16]) that this view lacks plausibility since it follows that (38) and (39) are *not* about the one thing, the Morning Star, but about two quiet different things which merely "happen" to have the same name.

Moreover, Rapaport's view can be interpreted in two ways, both of which lead to more serious problems. It may be interpreted as either

---

[4]Rapaport allows that it might be discovered that the two Morning Stars are co-extensive, in which case they are linked using the EQUIV/EQUIV case frame.

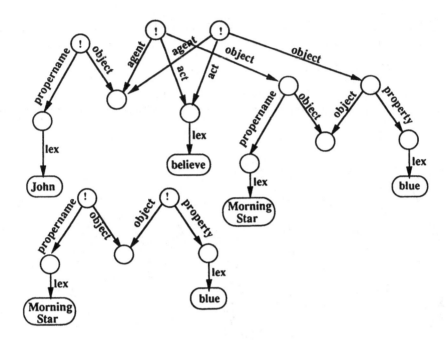

Figure 2: Rapaport's Representations of (38) and (39)

(A)   *Every de dicto* sentence introduces a new base node.

(B)   Only the **first** *de dicto* sentence (containing a given referring expression) introduces a new base node.

Interpretation **A** can be rejected on the ground that from the two sentences,

(40)   John believes that the Morning Star is blue,

and

(41)   John believes that the Morning Star is the Evening Star,

it would no longer follow that

(42)   John believes that the Evening Star is blue,

since it would not be the same Morning Star in each case.

Interpretation **B** leads to a more subtle problem. It will not always be possible to tell whether a given piece of network was produced via a *de dicto* sentence or via a *de re* sentence, and hence not always possible to tell whether a new node should be introduced or not. Compare the sets of sentences, S_1 and S_2

(S₁)   The Morning Star is blue.
Of the Morning Star, John believes that it is blue.
Of the Morning Star, John believes that it is named *the Morning Star*.

(S₂)   John believes that the Morning Star is blue.
(John's) Morning Star is blue and is named *the Morning Star*.

The two sets generate the same network (on Rapaport's theory), which given in Figure 3.

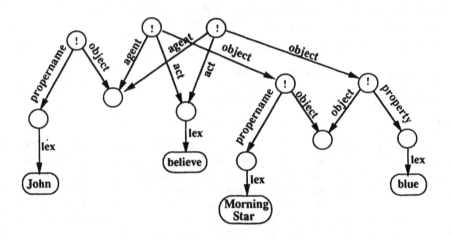

Figure 3: Representation of S₁ and/or S₂.

If, assuming interpretation **B**, CASSIE is told

(43)   The Morning Star is blue,

new network would be added if she had been told the sentences in S₂, but not if she had been told those in S₁. But there is no way to tell merely from the network which set of sentences generated it and so no way to tell whether or not a new base node need be created.

In place of Rapaport's theory then, a *de dicto* sentence will, by default at least, introduce a new base node only if the referring expression is completely new for CASSIE, only if she has never heard that name before. If CASSIE is already acquainted with a name, then she needs specific *evidence* that some new occurrence of that name does *not* refer to the same thing as do the earlier occurrences. It is that evidence which then allows her to distinguish between the two nodes bearing the same name. But without such evidence, she would in general be unable to tell them apart; and so without such evidence, there should be just one base node.

4.1.2   Second Difficulty

This difficulty with Rapaport's representations of beliefs emerges when two distinct matters are considered together; viz.,

(A)   How the EQUIV/EQUIV case frame is used in general.

(B)   The fact that Rapaport's theory treats a *de dicto* belief as consisting more or less of two beliefs that are held separately and independently, instead of as a *single* belief of two separate propositions.

Each matter is considered in turn before the second difficulty itself is examined.

The first matter, **A**, concerns Rapaport's representation, shown in Figure 4, of

(44)   The Morning Star is blue,

(45)   John believes that the Evening Star is blue,

and, to secure the identity of the "two" Morning Stars,

(46)   John's Evening Star is the Morning Star.

What is the relation between nodes m2 and m4? On the one hand, one might hold, in virtue of the equivalence of b1 and b2, that m2 and m4 represent the very same proposition. If m4 were asserted, there would be no new sentence that CASSIE could utter; in virtue of m2, she already believes that b2 is blue. Indeed, m4 should, on pain of inconsistency, actually *be* asserted. As far as CASSIE's beliefs are concerned, b1 and b2 may as well be merged to a single node (cf. Madia and Shapiro [8]). On the other hand, one might hold that m2 and m4 represent quite different propositions. After all, m2 is about b1, whereas m4 is about b2, which is supposed to represent a quite different thing. What needs to be decided is whether an *extensional* occurrence of *the Morning Star* refers to b1, or to b2, or indiscriminately to either. This question will be returned to shortly.

The second matter, **B**, concerns the fact that Rapaport represents propositions jointly believed, as being separately and independently believed. In particular, the *de dicto* belief

(47)   John believes that the Morning Star is blue,

is represented as two *separate* beliefs; viz., as

(48)   Of the Morning Star, John believes that it is it is blue, and of the Morning Star, John believes that it is named *the Morning Star*,

instead of as

(49)   Of the Morning Star, John believes both that it is named *the Morning Star* and that it is blue.

Putting **A** and **B** together allows the second of our two main difficulties to be stated.

Consider Rapaport's representations of

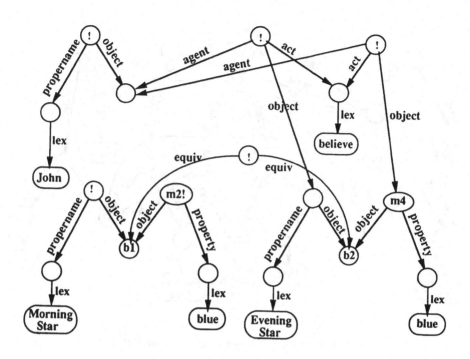

Figure 4: Rapaport's Representation of (44) – (46).

(50)   The Morning Star is blue.

(51)   John believes that the Evening Star is blue.

(52)   John's Evening Star is the Morning Star.

(53)   Of the Morning Star, John believes that it is bright.

Figure 5 shows Rapaport's representations of (50) – (52) together with two alternatives representation of (53), which are shown by the dotted lines.

    The difficulty is now straightforward. Alternative 2, but not alternative 1, licenses CASSIE to report

(54)   John believes that the Evening Star is bright,

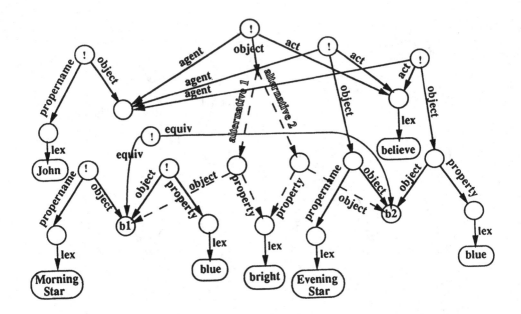

Figure 5: Rapaport's Representation of (50) – (53).

even though (54) does follow from the sentences given. Rapaport's theory therefore *requires* that an extensional occurrence of *the Morning Star*, as in (53), refer to b1, rather than to b2. In other words, it must favour alternative 1 over alterative 2 as the representation of (53). But what reason could be given for doing so?

One possible reason might be that an extensional occurrence of a name, such as *the Morning Star* in (53), refers to the base node connected to the name via the arc

(lex- proper-name- object).

This must be rejected, for in that case, if instead of (53), we considered the extensionally equivalent proposition

(55)   Of the *Evening* Star, John believes that it is bright,

then the representation would now be as per alternative 2, and the invalid inference to (54) would now be licensed after all.

A second possible reason might be that *the Morning Star* in (53) refers to the thing that *CASSIE*, not John, holds to be named *the Morning Star*. But, b1 and b2 are *equally* the thing that CASSIE holds to be so named. There is no general way for the network to remember that b1 was created to represent one of CASSIE's concepts, but b2 was created to represent (one of CASSIE's concepts of) one of John's concepts.

4.2 A Revised Representation of Propositional Attitudes

There are three intermingled sources of the difficulties for Rapaport's theory: the introduction of a new base node in representing belief sentences in the *de dicto* sense; the seductive effect of having base nodes which are "extensionally equivalent" but which, because they are not merged into a single node, tempt one into thinking that an extensional occurrence of a term can refer to one but not the other; and the representation of beliefs the agent holds jointly as if he held them singly.

To solve these difficulties, the following ideas are adopted

(I)   A sentence in the *de dicto* sense will not automatically introduce a new base node. A new base node will be introduced only if CASSIE has specific evidence that the object the *de dicto* sentence is about is one she was not previously acquainted with.

(II)   Multiple beliefs expressed by a single sentence, as in the case of a sentence in the *de dicto* sense, will be represented so as to include the fact that the beliefs are jointly or simultaneously held.

The following methodological principle is also adopted

(III)   No representation should make essential use of the EQUIV/EQUIV case frame. It should make no difference whether nodes linked by the EQUIV/ EQUIV case frame are merged into a single node or not. This remains true even when there are opaque contexts at issue. But, to avoid the seductive effect above, merging is highly recommended[5].

The new representation of the *de re* sentence

(56)   Of the Morning Star, John believes that it is blue,

is given in Figure 6, and of the *de dicto* sentence

(57)   John believes that the Morning Star is blue,

in Figure 7. This figure shows how the two beliefs contained in (57) are jointly or simultaneously held: m3 represents the fact that the propositions m1 and m2 jointly held. By locating the TYPE of an act *below* the point at which acts, or sub-acts, are joined, propositional attitudes other than belief can be similarly represented while maintaining the fact that the propositions are jointly held (cf. [11]). Figure 8 shows the representation of

(58)   John fears that the Morning Star is blue.

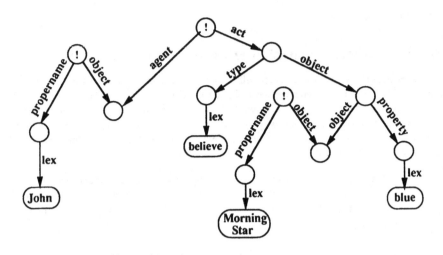

Figure 6: New Representation of (56).

Figure 9 shows the representation of the sentences that caused the problem for Rapaport's theory; viz., (50) – (53). The figure is presented assuming that after (52), the base nodes representing the Morning Star and the Evening Star have been merged, as recommended by III. In order for CASSIE to be able to infer (54), she would have to jointly hold m1 and m5, which she clearly does not. Inference is controlled by, to put it roughly, transitivity of "jointly held". For CASSIE to be able to infer from (51) that

(59)   John believes that the Morning Star is blue,

it is enough that she know

(60)   John believes that the Morning Star is the Evening Star.

Figure 10 shows the representations of (51) and (60), from which (59) follows by transitivity of "jointly held". To put it roughly: m10 represents John's belief that m1 and m2, and m11 represents John's belief that m2 and m3, from which we permit the inference to John's belief that m1 and m3.

4.3   An Extension of the Theory

The above approach is easily extended to apply to things other than ordinary objects, such as concepts and properties. The *de re* and *de dicto* senses of a sentence thus become merely the

---

[5]The use of the EQUIV/EQUIV case frame is thus merely an issue of whether network should or should not be simplified by merging, and this is at best a minor representation issue.

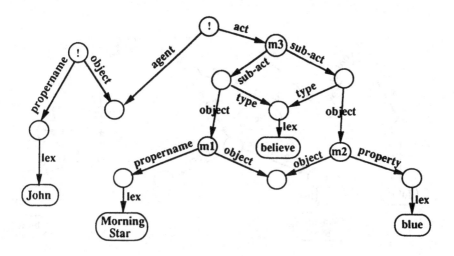

Figure 7: New Representation of (57).

extremes of a range of cases. Suppose that *XX-er* is an adjective meaning that someone has XX chromosomes, and so is extensionally equivalent to *female*. Below is a range of cases, which the extended theory can handle.

(61)   Henry VIII believes that Lady Jane is female,

where Henry is acquainted with *Lady Jane* and *female*,

(62)   Henry VIII believes that the fourteenth queen before Elizabeth II is female,

where he is acquainted with only *female*, and

(63)   Henry VIII believes that the fourteenth queen before Elizabeth II
         is an XX-er,

where he is not acquainted with either term.

4.4   Intensional Transitive Verbs

It is also easy to extend the approach to the intensional, transitive verbs so that both senses of:

(64)   John loves Mary.

can be represented; viz.,

(65)   Of Mary, John loves her,

(66)   Of Mary, John *both* loves her and believes that she is named *Mary*.

The representations parallel those of the propositional attitudes.

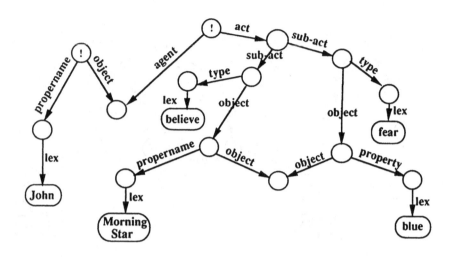

Figure 8: Representation of (58).

5 Opacity of the Second Kind

The logic of the attributive adverbs and the intensional sentences really is quite different from that of the propositional attitudes and the intensional, transitive verbs. Given that:

> (67)   John swam the river quickly,

and that

> (68)   John's swimming of the river is identical with John's crossing of the river.

there simply is no other sentence, S, which, together with (1) and (2), would allow CASSIE to infer[6]

> (69)   John crossed the river quickly.

Because of this difference, quite different representations are provided. The central idea is to represent attributive adverbs using intensional entities, entities which CASSIE holds are governed by non-extensional logic. Thus, though

> (70)   John swam the river quickly,

and

> (71)   John crossed the river slowly,

there will be nothing that is both quick and slow.

---

[6]Except, of course, such S as would *alone* entail (69).

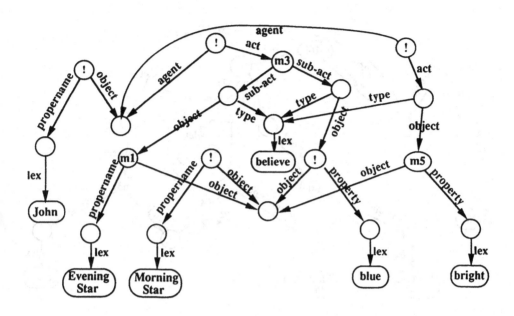

Figure 9: New Representation of (50) – (53).

5.1 Aspects

The intensional objects to be used in our representations are called *aspects*, which are reminiscent of Frege's *senses* [7] . Given a description, d, the Fregean sense associated with it is the *meaning* of d. The aspect associated with d, however, is the result of conceiving of the thing d refers to as, or *qua*, a thing to which the description d applies. Aspects are *objects*, albeit intensional, abstract objects. The general form of an aspect is:

aspect := *object*, qua *description true of the object*

In Wyatt [16] this intuitive notion of "qua" is replaced formally using Church's λ–abstraction [3].

5.2 Attributive Adverbs

There has been a considerable amount of work done on the nature of adverbial modification. By and large, there have been two main approaches. The first derives from Davidson's work on the logical form of action sentences [6] and treats adverbial phrases as representing properties of *events*. The second and more common approach treats adverbial as making complex predicates out of a simple ones. According to this approach, the adverb *quickly* in

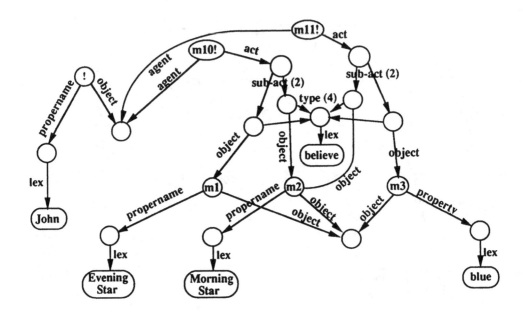

Figure 10: Representation of (51) and (60), from which (59) follows.

(72)   John runs quickly

operates on the predicate *runs(x)* to form the *complex* predicate *(quickly(runs))(x)* which is then predicated of John. This approach is favoured by Clark [4], Parsons [13], Montague [9], Thomason and Stalnaker [14], and Cresswell [5]. In this paper, the first approach is followed because the second, though able to accommodate the attribute adverbs, is not able to accommodate the intensional sentences, which, part of my claim is, have the same logical form as the attributive adverbs.

5.2.1 Davidson's Theory of Action

Davidson is concerned with the logical form of action sentences, and in particular, with adverbial modification. He explicitly excludes "intentional" adverbs such as *deliberately*, because they impute intentions to the agent, and "attributive" adverbs such as *quickly*, because of the very inference failures diagnosed above as stemming of opacity. Thus, he considers only sentences in which the action is modified by adverbial phrases, as in

(73)   John swam the river near the rapids.

Davidson holds that (73) entails *as a matter of logical form*

(74)   John swam the river.

His aim is to capture enough of the internal structure of (73) to reveal such entailments.

According to Davidson, verbs of action contain an extra place which refers to the *event* that the verb is then said to be about. Thus, (73) has the logical form

(75)   There is an event e such that e is a swimming, e was done by Jones, e was done to a river, and e was done near the rapids.

In this form, the entailments to the more simple sentences are straightforward. The representation of (73) is in Figure 11. The fact that (73) entails (74) is evident from the fact that the representation of (73) includes that of (74).

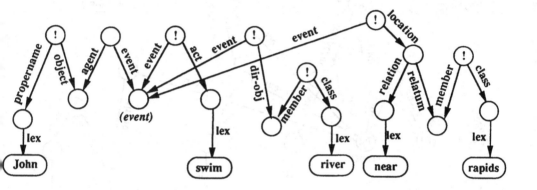

Figure 11: Representation of (73).

5.2.2   The Representation of Adverbs

The sentence containing an attributive adverb

(76)   John swam the river quickly,

is understood as having the logical form

(77)   There is someone b1 named *John*, there is an action b2 that is a swimming, and there is an object b3 that is a member of the class of rivers, such that b1 is the agent of b2, and b2 has b3 as its direct object, and there is an aspect a1 — b2, qua m1 — which is quick.

Assuming that John's swimming of the river is the *same* event as his crossing of the river, and that

(78)   John crossed the river slowly,

the representations of (76) and (78) are as in Figure 12. No inferences from the properties of an aspect to properties of the object the aspect is an aspect of, are permitted. Thus, nothing is said to be both quick and slow, since a1 (i.e., b2, qua being a swimming) is a different aspect from a2 (i.e., b2, qua being a crossing). (Details are in Wyatt [16].)

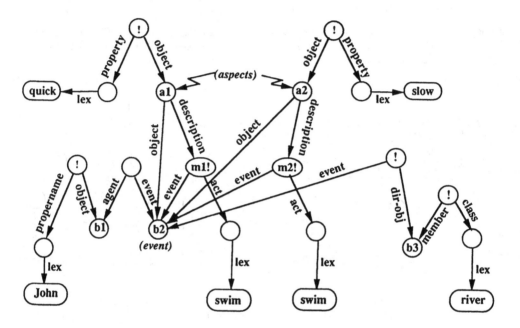

Figure 12: Representation of (76) and (78).

5.3   Intensional Sentences

Finally, intensional sentences are represented in terms of aspects, too. Consider again

(79)   The Morning Star is blue,

understood as an *intensional* sentence; that is, so that it is *not* inconsistent with

(80)   The Evening Star is red,

(81)   The Morning Star is the Evening Star,

and

(82)   Nothing is both blue and red.

In this intensional sense, (79) is understood as having the logical form

(83)   The Morning Star, qua thing named "Morning Star", is blue,

and is represented in Figure 13.

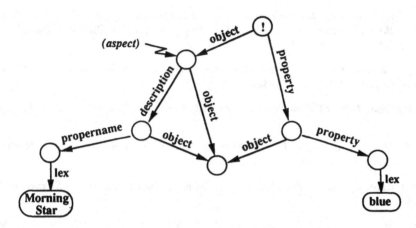

Figure 13: Representation of (79).

6 Conclusion

An examination of various opaque sentences reveals that their logic is far from uniform. The central difference discussed turned on whether or not the inferences that fail because of the opacity can succeed if further information is available. The propositional attitudes and the intensional, transitive verbs are of the first kind. The attributive adverbs and the intensional sentences are of the second kind. The logical form of the two kinds were given distinct representations.

References

[1] John Barnden. Imputations and Explications: Representational Problems in Treatment of Propositional Attitudes. *Cognitive Science*, 10:319–364, 1986.

[2] Roderick M. Chisholm. Intentionality. In P. Edwards, editor, *Encyclopedia of Philosophy*, pages 210–204. Macmillan and Free Press, New York, 1967. Volume 5.

[3] Alonzo Church. *The Calculus of Lambda Conversions*. Princeton University Press, Princeton, 1944.

[4] R. L. Clark. Concerning the Logic of Predicate Modifiers. *Noûs*, 4:311–335, 1970.

[5] M. J. Cresswell. *Adverbial Modification*. Reidel, Dordrecht, 1985.

[6] Donald Davidson. The Logical Form of Action Sentences. In Donald Davidson, editor, *Essays on Actions and Events*, pages 105–148. Clarendon Press, Oxford, 1980.

[7] Gottlob Frege. On Sense and Reference. In Peter Geach and Max Black, editors, *Translations from the Philosophical Writings of Gottlob Frege*, pages 56–78. Blackwell, Oxford, 1970. Originally published in 1892.

[8] Anthony S. Maida and Stuart C. Shapiro. Intensional Concepts in Propositional Semantic Networks. *Cognitive Science*, 6:291–330, 1982.

[9] R. M. Montague. *Formal Philosophy*. Yale University Press, New Haven, 1974. R. H. Thomason (ed.).

[10] Robert C. Moore. Problems in Logical Form. In *Proceedings of the 19th Annual Meeting of the Association for Computational Linguistics*, 1981.

[11] William J. Rapaport. Logical Foundations for Belief Representation. *Cognitive Science*, 10:371–422, 1986.

[12] William J. Rapaport, Stuart C. Shapiro, and Janyce M. Wiebe. Quasi-Indicators, Knowledge Reports and Discourse. Technical Report 96-15, State University of New York at Buffalo, Department of Computer Science, 1986.

[13] Terence Parsons. Some Problems Concerning the Logic of Grammatical Modifiers. In D. Davidson and G. Harman, editors, *Semantics of Natural Languges*, pages 127–141. Reidel, Dordrecht, 1972.

[14] R. H. Thomason and R. C. Stalnaker. A Semantic Theory of Adverbs. *Linguistic Inquiry*, 4:195–220, 1975.

[15] William A. Woods. What's in a Link: Foundations for Semantic Networks. In D. G. Bobrow and A. M. Collins, editors, *Representation and Understanding*, pages 35–79. Academic Press, New York, 1975.

[16] Richard W. Wyatt. The Representation of Opaque Contexts. Technical Report 89-14, 1989.

Design of an Emotion Profiler Using SNePS*

Charles Rapp
Martha Evens
Illinois Institute of Technology

David Garfield
UHS/Chicago Medical School

Abstract

SNePS is being used to implement an emotion profiler which is based on a new emotion theory. The system is designed to read a transcript of an actual doctor/patient conversation and produce a profile of the patient's emotional state. Because conversations are not restricted in topic and patients use words idiosyncratically, the emotion profiler's use of knowledge is limited. This paper describes a design and SNePS implementation which uses domain-independent knowledge to effectively parse and process transcripts.

1   Introduction

The first question that comes to mind with the title of this paper is, "What is an emotion profiler?" In terms of input and output, an emotion profiler reads a transcript of doctor/patient conversation and produces a list of the patient's emotions together with the emotion's intensity. The emotion profiler is based on a new theory proposed by [1]. This theory views emotions as the result of combining goals with events, standards with agents of events, and attitudes with objects. This theory lends itself to automation since the above information can be gleaned from text, as opposed to other theories which describe how emotion in terms of facial expression and gestures[2] or are produced from physiological processes within the brain [3]. This theory does build upon previous theories which discuss how emotions are produced when goals succeed, fail, or are unresolved[4, 5].

The work being describe here is not unique; previous systems have dealt with emotion representation: PARRY, BORIS, and FEELER. PARRY[6] modeled a paranoid mind and, utilizing an emotion theory by Izard[7], tracked the intensities of eight primary emotions. These emotions were then used to guide PARRY's response to a doctor's question and comment. BORIS[8] read stories concerning divorce and use emotion words (e.g., glad, grateful, and surprised) together with their situational context to deduce a character's goals. This work used Roseman's goal-oriented model of

*This investigation was supported by BRSGS07RR05366-28 awarded by the Biomedical Research Support Grant Program, Division of Research Resources, National Institutes of Health.

affect[4]. FEELER[9] was an emotion simulator which started with a goal graph and initial arousal level and then produced a list of emotions (and consequent arousal level) in response to the events it was fed.

This emotion profiler is being developed to provide a consistent and objective analysis of patient speech content. By comparing a verbal emotion profile with other non-verbal emotion measures[2], an accurate portrait of a patient's emotional state can be made. This in turn allows for testing theories which which explain emotional variations withn psychiatric syndromes.

Section two of this article explains how the emotion profiler works. An understanding of the knowledge constraints confronting this project makes it clear why SNePS was chosen to implement the emotion theory. The system uses three artificial intelligence (AI) technologies in a highly integrated environment: natural language processing, knowledge representation, and automated reasoning. SNePS provides all three technologies at the level of integration needed. How SNePS will be modified and used to implement the design is described in section three. Section four summarizes the project and offers suggestions concerning validation of the system.

2 Design

2.1 Knowledge Constraints

The driving concern of the design is the emotion profiler is limited in the knowledge it can apply to solving the problem. The conversations the profiler reads are not limited in topic and since no knowledge base yet exists across the breadth of human knowledge, the use of domain-specific knowledge is prohibitive. Even if such a knowledge base did exist, it would be of little use in processing schizophrenic communication, similar to the following quote[10]:

> Solenoiding people, storching people and all of that other garbage in giving the prestige of a romantic situation in lieu of cutting half of their fat supply or not giving them anything to drink or throwing them hard liquor before giving them soft liquor.

Trying to make sense of this nonsense, as a natural language understanding system must do, is a mistake. What does "solenoiding" or "soft liquor" mean? Attempting to extrapolate a meaning from the definition of solenoid is useless since that may not be what the patient intended at all. And even if that were possible, what use would that strategy be when the patient makes up words (neologisms), as in the case of "storching."

The next question is: How much knowledge can be used? This can be determined by propagating backwards from our goal of creating an emotion profile. To produce an emotion profile, the goals, standards, and attitudes of the patient are combined with events, agents of those events, and objects. What goals combine with what events, standards with agents, and attitudes with objects needs to be known. Combining attitudes and objects is readily done, given there is only one intensional representation of an object, as an attitude refers to either one particular object or class of objects. Likewise, standards refer to a particular agent or class of agents and a particular actions or class of actions (e.g., "Children should be seen not heard," or "John and Mary should get married.")

How to combine goals with events is currently an open issue. If domain-specific knowledge were available, the solution would be to expand the event into a causal network and create a plan for meeting the goal and then see if the event and its consequences would cause the plan to fail, succeed, or has no effect on the goal.

This problem is moot if the profiler is unable to find goals, standards, etc. in the text. Events, agents, and objects can readily be found in case frames[11]. Case frames define the number and kind of arguments associated with a verb. Examples of argument types are agent, instrument, experiencer, beneficiary, location and possessor. Objects are slot values, agent is in the agent slot, and events are those case frames which represent actions. Finding goals, standards, and attitudes are, however, beyond the province of case frames; instead, speech act theory can be utilized[12]. By understanding what the speaker is trying to accomplish with an utterance, the speaker's goals, standards, and attitudes become apparent. With this in mind, Searle developed a taxonomy of illocutionary acts which are differentiated according to the purpose of the utterance, the strength of the utterance, the speaker's status with regards to the hearer, etc.[13]. Searle's taxonomy consists of five classes:

Assertive The speaker, with varying degrees of belief and commitment, is stating the truth of the expressed proposition. "I think the coat is in the closet," and "John is lying!" are both assertives.

Directives The speaker is attempting to get the hearer to do something. "I would like it if you got your hair cut," would be a weak directive, while "Do your homework!" has greater strength. Questions are directives since the speaker is directing the hearer to supply information.

Commisives This illocutionary act commits the speaker to a future course of action. Promises are an example of a commisive.

Expressives The speaker expresses a psychological state concerning a state of affairs. Thanking and apologizing are expressives.

Declarations Because of the speaker's authority, just by making a statement, the propositional content becomes true. For example, when a monarch says, "I dub thee Sir John Smith," then John Smith is knighted, simply by the monarch's utterance.

By identifying the speech act, the goals, standards, and attitudes are made known. For example, in the directive, "Do your homework!", the speaker is expressing a goal of wanting the hearer to complete the homework assignment. The sentence, "John is a hog," expresses the speaker's attitude towards John.

One current issue is whether speech acts can be applied in a knowledge-weak manner. In the second example, if John is a human, then the speaker is asserting that John tends to take what he needs with no concern for others. Is it necessary to know that definition in order to understand that the metaphor is negative? Understanding indirect speech acts may indeed require domain-specific knowledge to be used. For that reason, sentences will be interpreted literally for this initial development. While this will cause emotion components (goals, standards, etc.) to be missed, it is considered an acceptable compromise in an already complex initial design.

Even so, there remains the problem of applying the basic speech act theory. One possible solution is to classify case frames according to speech act performed. This solution was hinted at when it was mentioned that events are case frames which represent actions. Another solution focuses on finding advice, warnings, promises, and threats by constructing partial practical arguments from text[14].

Underlying case frames is the idea of a physical object taxonomy. Such a classification is used by case frames to specify restrictions on the values which may fill slots. For example, one case frame for the verb write would specify that only objects in the class of writing utensils may fill the instrument slot and only an intelligent being can be the agent. Inheritance must be used to allow an object which is an member of a subclass of the required class to fill the slot. Finally, case frames require knowledge of English syntax (known as grammar) and word features, e.g., what part-of-speech a word belongs to or the tense of a verb (stored in a lexicon).

2.2 System Architecture

The knowledge used above can be grouped into two components:

1. The profiler which combines goals with events, standards with agents, and attitudes with objects to create the emotion profile;

2. Natural language processor which parsers the machine-readable transcript into case frames, using the grammar and lexicon.

Both of these components are built around the semantic memory, where the case frame templates, speech act knowledge, and lexicon are stored along with the results of each components work. The order of invocation is the opposite of the above order with the natural language processor first parsing the transcript, then the profiler finding the emotion components and combining them to create an emotion profile.

3 Implementation

The question "How does the emotion profiler work?" has been answered in terms of what steps the profiler takes to create an emotion profile and the knowledge needed by each step. The next question to be answered is, "How does each step apply that knowledge to achieve is task?" The answer to this question falls into the realm of implementation. Presented below is a description of how SNePS is used to implement each task and to represent the needed knowledge.

3.1 Natural Language Processor

Of the two components, the natural language processor is the most knowledge intensive. The knowledge used runs from morphological (needed for such works as "solenoiding"), through syntactic, to semantic. In other words, the natural language processor uses a lexicon, grammar, physical object taxonomy, and case frame templates. The actual process which uses this knowledge is the parser.

Choosing the type of parser to be used is simplified by the fact that SNePS provides an augmented transition network (ATN) parser, which is already integrated into the SNePS system.

3.1.1 Lexicon

The lexicon chosen for use in the emotion profiler is currently being developed as a joint project between IIT and the Virginia Polytechnic Institute[15]. The knowledge stored in the lexicon includes word features for nouns, irregular nouns, verbs, allowable modifiers for nouns and verbs, and list of synonymous words. Also included are physical object taxonomy and case frame templates. The taxonomy contains more that just a subclass-superclass relation; also identified are such relations as: part-whole, child-parent, female-sex, male-sex, etc. The case frame templates indicate for each verb argument its syntactic role (e.g., subject, direct object, indirect object, or prepositional object), case (agent, instrument, beneficiary, etc.), appearance restriction (obligatory, optional, or elliptical), and filler restriction. The knowledge for the lexicon is currently being collected from three machine-readable dictionaries (Websters' Seventh Collegiate Dictionary, Collins' English Dictionary, and Advanced Learners' Dictionary) and three word lists (Word Dictionary for Sager's Linguistic String Parser, Householder's Indiana Word Lists, and Brandeis Verb Lexicon)[16]. The size of the database is currently at 70,000+ words. The lexicon resides in a relational database. The work being done at the Virginia Polytechnic Institute is to convert this lexical database into semantic networks in SNePS[15].

3.1.2 Grammar

The RUS grammar[17] was chosen to provide the syntactic knowledge since it already is designed to work with an ATN parser and uses case frames to guide the parse. The idea behind the RUS parser is to interleave syntactic and semantic processing in an effort to reduce the amount of backtracking as much as possible. This interleaving is achieved by having the parser query the knowledge base about the validity of syntactic components. If the components agree with the semantics, the parser continues on the current path, pruning alternative paths; otherwise, the parser backtracks. RUS uses both a physical object taxonomy and case frames for validation: the taxonomy for making attachments to a noun, case frames for assigning roles at the clause level. When combined, these features make parsing deterministic in all but "garden-path" sentences.

RUS also employees such advanced features as a well-formed substring table (WFST) [18] and three word look-ahead[19] to reduce backtracking. A WFST is used to store syntactic constructs created by the parser, so in case the parser backtracks, the parser can check the WFST to see if the construct it is attempting to parse has been parsed before, avoiding duplication of effort. Three word look-ahead was first used in Marcus' PARSIFAL parser. when a parser reaches a choice point, instead of basing the choice branch on an hypothesis, the parser can look ahead up to three words. While three word look-ahead together with interleaved syntactic/semantic analysis does not completely remove backtracking from RUS, it does reduce it considerably.

The SNePS ATN will be extended to provide a well-formed substring table and three word look-ahead used by RUS. To implement the WFST, the push and pop arcs must be modified. Before the parser pushes to another network, it first checks if the parser has entered the same network at the same point in the text with the same registers and values by looking in the WFST. If so, the push arc advances to the point in text where the previous parse ended and returns the value found in the WFST. Otherwise, the push stores the position in text, the network being pushed, and the network's initial registers and their values are stored in system registers. If a pop arc for the network is reached, this information, along with the return value, is committed to the WFST. Three word look-ahead will be implemented as three functions, one for each word beyond the current point in text.

In turn, the RUS grammar must be extended to handle made up words, idiosyncrasies, and ambiguities. This requires placing arcs in the network for catching such parsing failures, determining why the parse failed, and taking the appropriate measures to correct the failure. This includes using morphology rules to handle gerundized nouns, a generic case frame for idiosyncrasies, or choosing among multiple cases in an ambiguous sentence.

One important feature of the natural language processor is the fact that it will generate only one intensional representation for each object mentioned in the transcripts. For example, if a patient talks about Tom and later mentions her boyfriend and Tom and her boyfriend are the same person, then only one node in the network will represent this person (in this case there are two extensions). By using only one intensional representation, case frames which refer to the same object are linked together. This fact is used by the profiler.

3.2   Profiler

The profiler will be implemented as SNePS rules, using forward-chaining, node-based and path-based reasoning to identify and combine emotion components. As shown in section 2.1, emotion components are found in instantiated case frames and speech acts. When the profiler finds corresponding components (e.g., an attitude and its corresponding object), it creates a network which states the emotion produced by these components and links the emotion to the components which produced it. When the text has been completely parsed, the emotions are then listed in chronological order.

In this case, chronological order means when the emotion's components were mentioned in text.

4   Summary

A system for automatically producing a profile of a person's emotional state from a machine-readable transcript of doctor/patient conversation is currently being developed as a joint project of IIT and the Chicago Medical School. Based on existing technology of natural language processing, knowledge representation, and automated reasoning and following on previous systems which dealt with emotion and its representation, the emotion profiler faces the challenge of finding the goals, standards, attitudes, events, agents, and objects mentioned in the conversation without the use of domain-specific knowledge. Given this constraint, it has been determined that an emotion profiler can be developed using case frames and knowlede-weak implementation of speech act theory. The emotion profiler will consist of two components: a natural language processor which translates text into case frames and speech acts, and a profiler which finds emotion components (goals, standards, etc.) and combines them to form the appropriate emotions. The natural language processor uses lexical, syntactic, and semantic (i.e., physical object taxonomy, case frames, and speech acts) knowledge for its task. The profiler uses knowledge to find emotion components in instantiated cases and speech acts and knowledge to combine emotion components, creating an emotion profile. Once built, the emotion profiler will be tested for consistency and validity. Consistency is tested by making sure the emotion profiler produces the same profile each time it reads the same transcript. Validation will be done by using human expert raters (psychiatrists and psychologists) who will assess the same transcripts for emotion content. An emotion token list, based on the same tokens found in Ortony, et. al. , will be used by the human raters to assess both the frequency and breadth of emotions. Comparison will then be made between human raters and the automatic emotion profiler.

References

[1] Ortony, A., G. Clore, A. Collins. *The Cognitive Structure of Emotions.* New York: Cambridge University Press, 1988.

[2] Ekman, P., W. V. Friesen. *Unmasking the Face.* Englewood Cliffs, N.J.: Prentice Hall, 1975.

[3] Tomkins, S. S. *Affect as the Primary Motivational System.* In M. B. Arnold (Ed.), Feelings and Emotions. New York: Academic Press, 1970.

[4] Roseman, I. *Cognitive Aspects of Discrete Emotions.* Doctoral Thesis, Yale University, 1982.

[5] Weiner, B. *The Emotional Consequences of Causal Ascriptions.* In M. S. Clark, S. T. Fiske (Eds.), Affect and Cognition: The 17th Annual Carnegie Symposium on Cognition. Hillside, NJ: Erlbaum, 1982.

[6] Colby, K. M. *Artificial Paranoia.* New York: Pergamon Press, 1975.

[7] Izard, C. E. *The Face of Emotion.* New York: Appleton-Century-Crofts, 1972.

[8] Dyer, M. G. *In-Depth Understanding.* Cambridge, MA: The MIT Press, 1986.

[9] Pfeifer, R. *Formalisierung in der Psychologie mit Hilfe von Computersimulation unter besonderer Berücksichtigung von Techniken der 'Künstlichen Intelligenz' - Forschung.* Doctoral Thesis, Swiss Federal Institute of Technology, 1979.

[10] Personal communication, 1989.

[11] Fillmore, C. J. *The Case for Case Reopened.* In P. Cole and J. Sadok (Eds.), Syntax and Semantics 8: Grammatical Relations. New York: Academic Press, 1977.

[12] Searle, J. R. *Speech Acts.* New York: Cambridge University Press, 1969.

[13] Searle, J. R. *Expression and Meaning.* New York: Cambridge University Press, 1979.

[14] Donaghy, K. *Recognizing Advice, Warnings, Promises, and Threats in Natural Language Settings.* Technical Memorandum, Department of Computer Science: Rochester Institute of Technology, 1989.

[15] Fox, E. A., J. T. Nutter, T. Ahlswede, M. Evens, J. Markowitz. *Building a Large Thesaurus for Information Retrieval.* In Proceedings of the Second ACL Applied. Austin, TX: Association for Computational Linguistics, 1988.

[16] Evens, M., S. Pin-Ngern, T. Ahlswede, S. M. Li, J. Markowitz. *Acquiring Information form Informants for a Lexical Database.* In U. Zernik (Ed.), Proceedings of the First International Lexical Acquisition Workshop. Los Altos, CA: Kaufmann, 1989.

[17] Bobrow, R. J. *The RUS System* (Technical Report 3878). Cambridge, MA: Bolt, Beranek, and Newman, Inc., 1978.

[18] Kay, M. *Algorithm Schemata and Data Structures in Syntactic Processing.* In B. J. Grosz, K. S. Jones, B. L. Webber (Eds.), Readings in Natural Language Processing. Los Altos, CA: Morgan Kaufmann, 1986.

[19] Marcus, M. P. *A Theory of Syntactic Recognition for Natural Language.* Cambridge, MA: The MIT Press, 1980.

Implications of Natural Categories for Natural Language Generation

Ben E. Cline and J. Terry Nutter
Department of Computer Science
Blacksburg, VA 24061
nutter@vtopus.cs.vt.edu

Abstract

Psychological research has shown that natural taxonomies contain a distinguished or basic level. Adult speakers use the names of these categories most frequently and can list a large number of attributes for them. They typically cannot list many attributes for superordinate categories and list few additional attributes for subordinate categories. Because natural taxonomies are important to human language, their use in natural language processing systems appears well founded. In the past, however, most AI systems have been implemented around uniform taxonomies in which there is no distinguished level. It has recently been demonstrated that natural taxonomies enhance natural language processing systems by allowing selection of appropriate category names and by providing the means to handle implicit focus. We propose that additional benefits from the use of natural categories can be realized in multi-sentential connected text generation systems. After discussing the psychological research on natural taxonomies that relates to natural language processing systems, the use of natural categorizations in current natural language processing systems is presented. We then describe how natural categories can be used in multiple sentence generation systems to allow the selection of appropriate category names, to provide the mechanism to help determine salience, and to provide for the shallow modeling of audience expertise. A SNePS-2.1 network and grammar is then described that generates descriptions of microcomputers from a natural taxonomy. This program illustrates salience determination and shallow modeling of audience expertise in a multiple sentence generation system.

1 Introduction

People represent information about kinds in taxonomies which are not uniform [RMG+76],[MR81]. In these natural taxonomies, one level of abstraction, called the *basic level,* is the most important and carries the most information. Adult speakers use basic level category names most frequently, and they are able to list large numbers of attributes for categories at this level. Since natural taxonomies form a fundamental basis underlying human language, it is important that natural language understanding and generation systems model them.

The use of natural categories in natural language understanding systems and in single sentence question and answer systems has been demonstrated [PS87] [PSR88]. Benefits include the ability to use appropriate category names and to handle implicit focus. We argue in this paper that the use of natural categories is also important in natural language generation systems that produce multi-sentence texts. In addition to allowing selection of appropriate category names, use of a natural taxonomy provides a mechanism to help determine salience, and provides for shallow but potentially useful modeling of audience expertise.

The structure of this report is as follows. Section 2 presents a brief overview of categorization theory results that relate to natural language generation. Section 3 reviews natural language understanding systems that use natural categories. Finally in Section 4, the enhancements to natural language generation systems that can be derived from the use of natural categories are outlined.

2   Theory of Natural Categories

A category is a collection of nonidentical objects or events that an organism treats as equivalent for some given context. Organisms divide their environment into categories in order to deal efficiently with the vast amount of information presented to them. Taxonomies are collections of categories organized by class inclusion. In a uniform taxonomy, no level is distinguished and attributes are placed at the level of maximal coverage. Although most AI systems model categorizations using a uniform taxonomy, psychologists have argued that one level of natural taxonomies is distinguished [RMG+76]. Categories at this basic level are the most cognitively efficient, carry the most information, and are those categories most differentiated from one another. Members of a basic level category have the most attributes in common. Tversky and Hemenway [1984] argue that basic level objects are distinguished mostly by part attributes, while members of subordinate classes tend to share parts and differ on other attributes.

For example, a typical biological taxonomy has basic level categories for both cats and dogs. Superordinate categories for these basic level categories include *mammal* and *animal*. The basic level categories have subordinate categories for particular breeds. Since members of basic level categories have the most attributes in common, a manx and a Maine ring-tail coon cat will have more attributes in common than either one has with a collie. Two subordinate categories of a basic level category will share many features. In addition, they have some additional features that distinguish them. For example, the *manx* subordinate category has the attribute *has short fur*, while *maine coon* has the attribute *has long fur*. But both subordinate categories share all the common features associated with felines.

Researchers have performed a variety of experiments to verify the existence of basic level categories. It was found that subjects list the greatest number of attributes for categories at the basic level. Few attributes are listed for superordinate categories, and few additional attributes are listed for subordinate categories [RMG+76]. It was also found that basic level categories were the most general level at which averaged shapes (produced by overlaying normalized shapes of category members) could be recognized, thus demonstrating that basic level categories are the highest categories for which a concrete mental image of all category members can be formed. For example, subjects could recognize averaged shapes for basic level categories such as dog and chair but not for superordinate categories such as mammal and furniture [RMG+76]. Tests were also performed to verify that basic level categories are the most inclusive for which highly similar sequences of motor movements are made to objects in the category [RMG+76].

However, the most important results for this discussion relate basic level categories to language. Without some categorization system, we would need a separate word for each unique item in the world including each blade of grass and each insect. Natural categories provide a way out of this dilemma; as a result they have had a fundamental influence on human language. Regularities in classification across languages have been uncovered [TH84]. Although category cuts were originally thought to be arbitrary, these regularities appear to be linked to structure in the perceived world. Experiments by [RMG+76] have demonstrated that the names associated with the basic level categories are those most used by adults and first used by children. The basic level is the one at which adults spontaneously name objects.

Classically, it was thought that category membership was established by necessary and sufficient criteria. More recent research has focused on graded category membership [MR81],[SM81]. Some exemplars of a category are highly representative while others are less so. For example, most birds have feathers and fly. However, penguins are members of the basic level category bird, but they are atypical in their flying ability. One line of research claims that the most representative exemplars may be used as prototypes for determining class membership [SM81].

Finally, categorization research has pointed out that although principles by which we decide which categories are at the basic level are expected to be universal, for a given domain, the basic level category itself may not be universal [MR81], [RMG+76]. Both expertise and cultural significance of the domain affect the selection. The level of expertise also affects the amount of information associated with the basic and subordinate levels. It is believed that an expert's knowledge is often confined to specific parts of the taxonomy, thereby creating unevenness in the taxonomy. There also appears to be a level below which basic level categories cannot be formed regardless of the frequency of use or level of expertise due to the lack of attributes to differentiate objects.

3 Applications of Categories in Natural Language Understanding

Peters and Shapiro [1987] have implemented a semantic network system for natural language understanding that models natural category systems. In their representation, a member/class case frame is used to describe the inclusion of an object in a basic level category. In addition, ISA case frames are used to designate objects as members of subordinate and superordinate categories. The category hierarchy is built from subclass/superclass case frames. In this system, there is not a great deal of inheritance in the hierarchy. Instead, most inheritance occurs between basic level categories and members of these categories.

One of the most important results of using this representation is that this system is able to choose the most appropriate category name for an object in answers to questions. For example, knowledge in the system indicates that cat is a basic level category. The system was told that Jane petted a manx, a manx is a cat, a cat is a mammal, and mammals are animals. When asked who petted an animal, it answered that Jane petted a cat. This response is deemed more appropriate than the responses "Jane petted a manx" or "Jane petted an animal." Violations of this rule can produce unintended humor: compare "Jane petted the cat" with "Jane petted the carnivore."

Peters, Shapiro, and Rapaport [1988] describe an extended version of this system in which context affects the attributes associated with basic level categories. For example, in the context of farm, cows, horses, and pigs are more typical of the category animal than lions and elephants. The reverse is true in the context of zoo. The system uses the context-independent and context-dependent information associated with basic level categories to guide focus while processing English text input. This technique enhances text understanding and anaphora resolution.

This system uses default generalizations to represent typical attributes of members of a basic level category. These generalizations are based on category part-whole structure and image schematic structure, other perceptual structure, and functional attributes. This information is useful in determining category membership and is the knowledge that forms the context-independent structure of the basic level categories.

The context-dependent structure associated with concepts is formed by thematic associates (concepts related to events) and by other concepts not related to categorization. Such information is only relevant in particular situations. For example, *mortgage* is a context-dependent concept associated with *house*. *Mortgage* is a useful concept when attempting to understand text concerning the purchase of a house. In understanding the sentences

Jane bought a house.

The mortgage was high.

the system adds the concept *mortgage* to a potential focus list when it parses the first sentence because the concept *mortgage* is a thematic associate of *house* in this situation. When "mortgage" is read in the second sentence, the system is able to relate this mortgage to the particular house that Jane bought by using the context-dependent knowledge triggered by the first sentence.

4   Natural Categories and Connected Text Generation

The AI system discussed above demonstrates that the use of natural categories enhances natural language understanding systems and single sentence question and answer systems. We propose that the use of natural taxonomies is also beneficial to natural language generation systems that produce multi-sentential output. Whether a generation system is producing descriptions of objects from a knowledge base or giving extended answers to questions about such objects, knowledge of basic level categories allows the system to produce more natural sounding and more widely understandable text due to the importance of natural taxonomies in psychology and linguistics.

4.1 Selecting Description Level

Since basic level category names are those most frequently used by adults and are widely understood, when describing an object or a subordinate class, a natural language generation system should define the item in terms of its basic level category. Names at the basic level provide the reader with the most information, as typical adults can list a large number of attributes for basic level categories. For example, in describing the subordinate category manx, a generation system should indicate that a manx is a breed of cat. References to superordinate categories (e.g. "The manx is a mammal" or "The manx is an animal") give the reader far less information.

A natural language generation system should also take into account the degree of representativeness of a member or subordinate category of a basic level category when generating qualifying terms [MR81]. Qualifying terms such as "true" or "technically" are typically applicable only to subsets of category exemplars. "True" is applicable to category members that are strongly typical, while "technically" is reserved for atypical members. "A collie is a true dog" is acceptable while "A collie is technically a dog" is not. "A bottle-nosed dolphin is a true whale" is odd at best while "A bottle-nosed dolphin is technically a whale" is a good description. One way of distinguishing atypical individuals or classes is by noting the absence of features typical of the basic kinds to which they belong. That is, bottle-nosed dolphins are atypical whales because they are roughly human-sized, while typical whales are much bigger. Wolves are technically dogs; Persians are true cats.

When describing a class or individual relative to another fixed superclass, selecting the correct modifier depends only on the detection of typicality or atypicality relative to the second class. Hump-backed whales are true whales, but only technically mammals. The usefulness of the distinguished basic level comes in when the system must describe a class or individual without having a fixed superclass supplied.

4.2 Identifying Salient Characteristics

Natural categories which contain a description of typical features can be used for determining salience. In existing generation systems, salience is typically determined by some static measure. For example, the TEXT system [McK85] is a question and answer system that is used to describe the structure and content of a database that contains descriptions of military hardware, e.g., ships and missiles. In TEXT "distinguishing descriptive attributes" are attribute-value pairs that are used to partition classes of entities into meaningful subclasses. The system also keeps track of attributes that are constant across subclasses. Distinguishing descriptive attributes and constant database attributes indicate important features in describing classes or in comparing and contrasting one class to another. This technique can be viewed as the application of a limited type of salience processing.

The use of distinguishing features to determine salience fails in general for two reasons. First, distinguishing features may not always be salient. Consider for example a comparison of two different computer systems. The serial numbers of the two systems distinguish them, but serial numbers are rarely salient (except in cases of inventory or theft). Serial numbers would never be included in a discussion of the relative merits of two particular machines. Second, distinguishing features of a category provide little additional information when describing a typical member of the category. The category *bird* contains the distinguishing attribute *can fly*. However, when describing a robin, to indicate that it can fly tells the average reader nothing he doesn't already know. On the other hand, it is an important feature of ostriches that they are birds that do not fly [Nut85], [Nut83].

As Peters, Shapiro, and Rapaport [1988] used default generalizations to describe basic level category attributes, we believe that these types of default rules are useful for determining salience in a connected text generation system. Because the attributes of basic level categories are familiar to most general readers, it is useless to mention them when describing an object that is strongly typical of the category. Sometimes mentioning the obvious can even imply unintended interpretations because the reader does not expect a speaker or writer to state the obvious unless it is important. On the other hand, when a subordinate category or a member of a basic level category has an attribute that differs from a basic level attribute, this difference is probably salient and is a candidate to be included in the system output. For example, if the particular cat that is being described has only three legs while a default rule of the basic level cat category indicates that cats typically have four legs, this difference has potential salience. If the cat has four legs, on the other hand, the system need hardly say so.

4.3   Shallow Expertise Model

Natural categories provide a way for a natural language generation system to model audience expertise [PS87]. In the domain of their expertise, experts tend to have a different taxonomy structure than nonexperts. The level of abstraction at which the basic level categories of an expert occur differs from that for nonexperts as does the amount of information at both the basic level categories and the subordinate categories. For example, Rosch *et al.* [RMG+76] discovered that one of their subjects was a former airplane mechanic. While *airplane* was a basic level category for other students, the former mechanic had basic level categories based on types of airplanes. Furthermore, this student was able to list many more attributes for the categories related to *airplane* than were other students.

Consider an author producing a paper for a meeting of cognitive scientists. The audience will contain a number of experts with varying degrees of expertise in various areas of the field. For the paper to be effective, the author must attempt to write it at a level of expertise that is common to the members of the audience, presenting his arguments in terminology common to the experts and using concepts that they share. If the author writes at a higher level of expertise than is common to the audience, the majority of them will not understand his paper. On the other hand, a paper at a lower level which explains commonly understood concepts will bore them.

In a similar manner, a generation system should tailor its output for a particular audience by modeling audience expertise. Where the audience is a large group, many of whose members are unknown, deep modeling of the audience individual-by-individual is clearly impossible. Furthermore, even if it were possible, it would not be appropriate, since it would be too computationally intensive to be usable. So a shallow mechanism is needed for determining the appropriate level of discourse for a particular audience. An implementation based on natural taxonomies can provide such a shallow model. In order to adjust a generation system for a more expert audience, the basic level categories would be moved to a lower level of abstraction and additional knowledge would be added to the basic and subordinate categories. Since the type of generation system we propose relates objects to their basic level category names, basic categories at a lower level of abstraction would cause the system to use more expert terminology. For example, a system modeling a feline expert would have breed categories at the basic level and would tend to use breed names when describing individual cats instead of the term *cat*. The addition of knowledge to the basic and subordinate categories would allow a generation system to produce text more suitable for experts. Although this technique allows a generation system to produce terminology at the appropriate level of expertise, techniques to select appropriate discourse styles based on the degree of expertise are also needed.

4.4 Demonstration

Two demonstration programs, each consisting of a semantic network knowledge base and an ATN grammar for language generation, were developed in SNePS-2.1 [SG89] to illustrate the use of basic level categories in natural language generation. The first program illustrates the use of salience rules based on typical features of a natural category, while the second deals with shallow modeling of audience expertise. In addition, these programs demonstrate selection of the appropriate description level by relating the item being described to its basic level category. Both use a representation similar to that of Peters and Shapiro [1987] to construct a natural taxonomy of microcomputers.

In the first demonstration, *microcomputer* is the basic level category. There are two subordinate categories, *IBM PC* and *Morrow*, with each subordinate containing an individual microcomputer. The individual Morrow belongs to John, while the IBM PC belongs to Mary. IBM PC's have keyboards and direct video interfaces and do not connect to terminals, while Morrow's do not have keyboards or direct video interfaces but do connect to terminals. IBM PC's have an 8088 microprocessor, while Morrow's have a Z-80. Both individual units have specific serial numbers and optional hard disk drives. There are a number of rules in the system that allow individual items to inherit properties from the categories to which they belong.

Typical features of the basic level category are represented by SNePS rules. In this demonstration, items belonging to the natural category *microcomputer* typically have keyboards, direct video interfaces, and serial numbers and typically do not connect to terminals. There are also rules that indicate if an item has a feature that differs from what is typical for the category to which it belongs, this fact is potentially salient. These rules allow our program to output that the Morrow does not have a keyboard or a direct video interface and connects to a terminal while remaining silent about the IBM PC's keyboard, direct video interface, and terminal connection. A reader who is familiar with the current low-end microcomputers would assume that a unit has both a keyboard and a direct video interface and that an additional terminal is not required for operation unless told otherwise. The salience rules also causes the program not to mention the units' serial numbers, or even the fact that they have serial numbers, since microcomputers typically have serial numbers.

Although the deviation of an item from the typicality of its basic level category can be used to discover potentially salient features, additional salience rules are required. There are some features

> (John owns a microcomputer. It is a Morrow which has a hard disk drive and a Z-80 microprocessor and does not have a direct video interface or a keyboard. It connects to a terminal.)
>
> (Mary owns a microcomputer. It is an IBM PC which has an 8088 microprocessor.)

Figure 1: Output of first demonstration program.

> (John owns a Morrow. It has a 64K memory and a 10M hard disk drive.)
>
> (Mary owns an IBM PC. It has a Color Graphics Adapter, a Color Monitor, a 20M hard disk drive and a 640K memory.)

Figure 2: Output of the second demonstration program.

which are either always potentially salient because they are central features of the category or they are salient in certain contexts. We represented that the microprocessor on which a microcomputer is based is a central feature and provided a rule to indicate that central features are potentially salient. Although serial numbers are rarely salient, they would certainly be in the context of a generation program used in a microcomputer inventory system. In such a system, the serial number of a computer would be represented as a central feature.

We also included rules that indicated that the existence on an individual computer of an optional feature is a potentially salient feature. For example, a hard disk drive is an optional feature on an IBM PC. It may therefore be worth noting that a particular IBM PC has a hard disk drive. In addition, rules were included to indicate that certain parameters associated with some features, when known, are potentially salient. For example, the fact that a microcomputer has a primary memory is not salient, but the amount of that memory is potentially salient.

Figure 1 gives the output of the first demonstration program when asked to describe John's Morrow and Mary's IBM PC. The program first relates the item to it's natural category and then outputs all the potentially salient features indicated by the rules described above.

The second demonstration illustrates how a shallow model of audience expertise can be built around a natural taxonomy. This program uses the same grammar as the first demonstration; however, the knowledge base was changed to correspond to an audience with greater expertise than the one for which the first program generated text. In this case, *Morrow* and *IBM PC* were made the natural categories and additional knowledge was added about the two individual microcomputers. The amount of primary memory and the size of the hard disk drive for each unit was added. The type of terminal to which the Morrow connects and the type of direct video interface and monitor that is part of Mary's IBM PC was also represented. Figure 2 is the output of the program when directed to describe John's and Mary's microcomputers. This output is intended for a more technical audience than the output of the first program. Since *Morrow* and *IBM PC* are basic level categories, it is assumed that the reader is familiar with the features of each brand (e.g., the microprocessor it is built around and whether or not it has a keyboard). In this program, the salient information is derived from the optional feature and optional value rules.

Three important observations should be made about these demonstrations. First, deviation from typicality is a useful salience rule; however, additional rules are needed to identify other potentially salient features. Second, in a larger program, these salience rules would produce too much information. Additional rules, based on style and discourse goals, would be needed to select a subset of the potentially salient information for surfacing. Third, although the shallow model of expertise can be used to select appropriate terminology for a particular audience, additional mechanisms are required to alter the discourse structure used in descriptions for different types of audiences [Par85]. A novice audience would require functional explanations of concepts which more expert audiences would already understand.

4.5 Conclusion

Current research has demonstrated the usefulness of natural category taxonomies in natural language understanding systems and in single sentence question and answer systems. We have argued that connected text generation systems can also benefit from the results of categorization research. Natural categories allow generation systems to produce more understandable text by describing objects and subordinate categories in terms of their basic level category names which are widely understood and have many attributes associated with them. Basic level categories also provide a way for a generation system to determine salient features of a knowledge base by providing typical attributes of basic level classes so that the atypical attributes of a member can be determined. The attributes of an object that differ from these defaults indicate potentially salient information. Modeling expertise by shifting basic level categories and attributes of subordinate categories and by adding additional knowledge to the categories can be used to have a natural language generation system produce text for different audiences.

Our future research will focus on additional enhancements to connected text generation systems that are possible through the use of natural taxonomies. We believe that natural categories can aid a generation system in the selection of discourse schema by indicating areas of the knowledge base where differences between objects may be located and that the use of a natural taxonomy provides increased efficiency of inheritance over uniform taxonomies by grouping attributes at the basic level and associating each object with its basic level category.

References

[McK85] K. R. McKeown. *Text Generation*. Studies in Natural Language Processing. Cambridge University Press, Cambridge, 1985.

[MR81] C. B. Mervis and E. Rosch. Categorization of natural objects. In M. R. Rosenzweig and L. W. Porter, editors, *Annual Review of Psychology*, volume 32, pages 89–115. Annual Reviews, Inc., 1981.

[Nut83]   J. T. Nutter. What else is wrong with non-monotonic logics? Representational and informational shortcomings. In *Proceedings of the Fifth Annual Conference of the Cognitive Science Society*, 1983.

[Nut85]   J. T. Nutter. Deciding what to say: The need for dynamic selection criteria in connected text generation. Technical Report 85-101, Tulane University Computer Science Department, 1985.

[Par85]   C. L. Paris. Description strategies for naive and expert users. In *Proceedings of the 23rd Annual Meeting of the Association of Computational Linguistics*, pages 238-245, Chicago, Ill., 1985.

[PS87]   S. L. Peters and S. C. Shapiro. A representation for natural category systems. In *Proceedings of the Tenth International Joint Conference on Artificial Intelligence*, pages 140-146, Los Altos, CA, 1987. Morgan Kaufman.

[PSR88]   S. L. Peters, S. C. Shapiro, and W. J. Rapaport. Flexible natural language processing and Roschian category theory. In *Proceedings of the Tenth Annual Conference of the Cognitive Science Socitey*, pages 125-131, 1988.

[RMG+76]   E. Rosch, C. B. Mervis, W. D. Gray, D. M. Johnson, and P. Boyes-Braem. Basic objects in natural categories. *Cognitive Psychology*, 8:382-439, 1976.

[SG89]   Stuart C. Shapiro and The SNePS Implementation Group. *SNePS-2.1 User's Manual*. Department of Computer Science, State University of New York at Buffalo, 1989.

[SM81]   E. E. Smith and D. L. Medin. *Categories and Concepts*. Harvard University Press, Cambridge, 1981.

[TH84]   B. Tversky and K. Hemenway. Objects, parts, and categories. *Journal of Experimental Psychology: General*, 113(2):169-191, June 1984.

Lecture Notes in Computer Science